Latin American Broadcasting

From Tango to Telenovela

Latin American Broadcasting

From Tango to Telenovela

Elizabeth Fox

UNIVERSITY *of*

LUTON PRESS

British Library Cataloguing in Publication Data
A catalogue record for this book is available from the British Library

ISBN: 1 86020 515 1

In Memory of Patricia Anzola, our friend

Published by
John Libbey Media
Faculty of Humanities
University of Luton
75 Castle Street
Luton
Bedfordshire LU1 3AJ
United Kingdom
Tel: +44 (0) 1582 743297; Fax: +44 (0) 1582 743298
e-mail: ulp@luton.ac.uk

Cover Design by Creative Identity, Hertford, UK
Typeset in Monotype Erhardt
Printed in Hong Kong by Da Hua Printing Co Ltd

Contents

Acknowledgments

My grateful thanks go to many people in Latin America and the United States for their help with this book. The research library at the United States Information Agency gave me access to their unique collection of historical information, which I used in Chapter 1 on the International Relations of Latin American Broadcasting. Hamid Mowlana, Lewis Goodman and the faculty of the School of International Service of the American University gave me invaluable guidance on many of the theoretical and policy issues within the broader field of development and international relations. My colleagues in Latin America, with whom I have shared the struggle for democratic media for over a quarter of a century, provided companionship and much of the raw data I used in the country chapters: Fatima Fernandez, Beatriz Solis, and Ruben Sergio Caletti in Mexico; Ingrid Sarti, Ana Maria Fadul, Sonia Moriera, Roberto Amaral, and José Marquez de Melo in Brazil; José Antonio Mayobre, Elizabeth Safar, Alejandro Alfonso, Oswaldo Caprilles and Antonio Pasquali in Venezuela; Luis Peirano, Rafael Roncagliolo, and Juan Gargurivich in Peru; Patricia Anzola and Jesus Martín in Colombia; Oscar Landi, Heliberto Muraro, and Silvio Wasibord in Argentina; Roque Faraone in Uruguay; Carlos Catalan, Giselle Munizaga, Paulina Gutierrez, Maria de la Luz Hurtado, and Valerio Fuenzalida in Chile; and Luís Ramiro Beltrán, who is hard to place in any country but ended up, as he started, in the Bolivian highlands.

Other Books by the same author

Dias de Baile: El Fracaso de la Reforma de la Televisión en América Latina, Mexico: FelaFacs, 1991.
Televisión y Democracia en América Latina, (with others) Lima: IPAL, 1989
Media and Politics in Latin America: the Struggle for Democracy, London: SAGE and Barcelona: G. Gili (Spanish), 1988.
TV y Comindad: Cinco Falacias, Santiago: CENECA, 1986.
Comunicación y Democracia en América Latina, (with others) Lima: DESCO, 1982.
Comunicación Dominada: los Estados Unidos en los Medios de América Latina, (with Luis Ramiro Beltran), Mexico: Nueva Imagen, 1980.

Introduction

Twentieth century Latin America proved fertile soil for radio and television broadcasting industries. The strong oral traditions and the exuberant humour of irreverence and complicity of the young, multi-racial societies provided ample content and talent for diverse programming. The music, drama, and news, transmitted over the airwaves by radio and television played to the dreams of the new nations and the loneliness of the migrants in the vast new cities. Growing metropolises and markets fuelled the expansion of the industry, often with the help of authoritarian leaders and spirited entrepreneurs. Radio and television broadcasting soon linked together nations and a continent, joined already by language, religion, and colonial history.

The imported technologies of radio and later television, however, did not arrive in a vacuum, nor did they come without baggage. When radio first appeared, the societies of Latin America had fast growing free-market economies with significant foreign investments. Local entrepreneurs had learned to use advertising to reach the elites as well as the surging masses of immigrants flocking to the cities to work in the factories. Most Latin American radio stations were conceived and born commercial, and many were set up by foreign radio manufacturers seeking to expand the markets for their products in Latin America.

The predominant model of broadcasting to reach Latin America was the privately owned, commercially operated industry forming in the United States. Many Latin American and US scholars[1] have attributed the evolution of Latin American broadcasting into one of the most commercially successful, monopolistic and undemocratic broadcasting industries in the world withto the pervasive influence in the region of the US government and broadcasting industries. Other scholars see this influence as having exerted an equally powerful but positive influence in the growth of Western-style commercial media in the region.[2]

While foreign influence was important, internal domestic factors were probably more important in determining the evolution of broadcasting in Latin America. Radio and television pushed aside existing forms of communication, reached new sectors of the population, and became important parts of people's lives and nation's economies. Broadcasting challenged government's control of information and obliterated older arts and cultures from an earlier, perhaps more authentic past. Latin American broadcasters made big profits, reached large audiences, and wield-

---

1 See (Beltrán and Fox 1980), (Dorfman and Mattelart 1970), (Mattelart 1970), (Schiller 1969, 1976), (Schwoch 1990), (Schnitman 1984), (Sinclair 1986), (Wells 1972).

2 For example, (Dizard 1966).

ed great power to engage public opinion and unify the tastes and images of many cultures and peoples into a standardised, mass-produced product. More than external influence, however, the economic, social, and political conflicts in these societies surrounding the introduction and growth of broadcasting, and the accommodations reached among the different domestic actors, largely defined the way radio and television evolved.

In some countries, the introduction of broadcasting was left in the hands of private developers and their foreign investors and suppliers. Early on, in other countries governments recognised the political power of the new sources of information and public opinion and attempted to place radio and television under state control. In still others, communication policies evolved haphazardly as business and political elites reacted to the growing economic and political influence of broadcasting media. Zig-zags between laissez-faire and authoritarian control of the media led to different arrangements among states, industry, and other actors, resulting in institutional and policy legacies that often were carried over into new phases of technological development of the media. These different arrangements and institutional developments paved the way for the monopolisation of domestic media resources, the lack of participation in the media by social actors, and the unequal balance between social service and commercial gain present in most media operations in Latin America. The domestic accommodations surrounding broadcasting in each country help explain why, despite similar foreign influences, some countries eventually developed private media industries with strong, autonomous political roles while in others the media remained politically fragmented and economically weak.

In this book I analyse the patterns of foreign and domestic conflict and accommodation that accompanied the introduction and growth of radio and television in Latin America and specifically in Argentina, Brazil, Chile, Colombia, Mexico, Peru, Uruguay, and Venezuela. I identify the similarities and differences that resulted in the present state of media development in the each country. By looking at more than one country and contrasting similar periods and conflicts over a period of time, I attempt to build a framework for understanding the patterns of domestic media policies and the role of international relations in Latin American broadcasting.

Historically, studies of broadcasting in Latin America have focused on the charismatic personalities of the media's founders or on the caprices of political leadership in a particular society. Studies have ignored the basic patterns of conflict of the state and the media, or between private media owners and social forces occurring in all societies.[3] From the beginning of radio in the first decades of the twentieth century to the late twentieth century preponderance of television, the relationship between the state, the media, and society in Latin American has changed in the direction of the increased autonomy and political power of the private broadcasting industries in relation to the state and civil society. The broadly chronological patterns and in some cases turning points in this relationship appear to be:

---

3 See for example (Brunner et al 1989), (Capriles 1980), (Cohen 1971 and 1989), (Federico 1982), (Hurtado 1989), (Gargurevich 1978 and 1990), (Miceli 1972), (Noguer 1985), (Pareja 1984), (Prada 1986), (da Silva 1986), (Sodre 1971 and 1981). A few studies have attempted to compare selected trends, like the development of national production capabilities in several countries (Portales 1987).

(1) The initial formative impact of foreign, mainly US, capital, technology, and creative talent on Latin American domestic radio industries in societies that already had developed markets for advertising and consumer goods and a positive image of US commercial broadcasting.

(2) The growth of populism and the need for the Latin American state to control the information and entertainment sources of the growing mass urban movements.

(3) During the second World War, the impact of state-directed efforts by the US Government, often working with US private broadcasters, to insure support for the Allied cause, and later a similar effort to combat the spread of communist ideologies.

(4) The failed efforts of the populist/redistributive state, faced with both domestic and foreign opposition, to bring broadcasting industries under national policy directives and insure a broader role in their operations for civil society.

(5) The liberalisation and transnationalisation of the media facilitated by the Latin American military dictatorships and liberal economic reforms of the 1970s and 1980s.

(6) The emergence of the monopolistic media industries as autonomous domestic political forces, aided by the weaknesses of political parties and of elected democratic governments.

An emerging seventh pattern, perhaps foreshadowing the decline of the Latin American domestic media monopolies, could result from increased competition in domestic markets from new foreign investors, including investment from other Latin American countries. The direct delivery of foreign satellite channels and the increased 'regionalisation' of broadcasting also could portend a decline in the economic and political power of the domestic media monopolies of Latin America.

The growth of monopolistic domestic broadcasting industries occurred in different degrees throughout Latin America, generally following the pattern of events outlined above. Certain factors like the influx of foreign capital and the influence of the US Government during the war occurred more or less at the same time in all countries. Other events occurred in the same sequence but with lapses of a decade or so while the media reached a critical size or domestic political forces developed a specific need to form and control public opinion.

The changes in the relationships of the state, media, and society from *laissez-faire* to media autonomy took place within the context of other transformations in Latin America: urbanisation; industrialisation; the decline of traditional political forces; and the growth of new political movements. The 'middle' years of growth of the media in Latin America were by and large marked by the emergence of an interventionist state, with an increasing role in social welfare and development, and by the evolution of a modern industrial sector of the economy. In some cases, this new and expanded state role made the state a mediator in the conflicts between different interests involving the media. In most, however, a stronger state led to increased tension between the state and media owners over the distribution of resources and access to information, news, and entertainment.

The failed efforts of Latin American states in the late 1960s and 1970s to institutionalise a redistributive or social welfare role for the domestic media and increase the role of civil society in media ownership made possible the growing autonomy of the media industries in their commercial operations. This commercial autonomy often came in exchange for the media's political docility and, in some cases, active support for authoritarian, non-democratic regimes. This autonomy, and the lack of state oversight or regulation allowed the private media industries to grow stronger, eventually becoming independent from state support, and, in some cases, taking an active role in selecting and deposing political leaders.

Much of the research on the Latin American media, especially on television, focuses on the importance of international relations, specifically exports of foreign capital, technology, news, and entertainment as explanations of how the domestic media industries developed in the region. My analysis of Latin American broadcasting does not ignore the importance of international relations in helping set the course of the development of the Latin American radio and television industries, a topic I explore in depth in the first chapter. I attempt, however, to bring to the role of international relations, an understanding of the domestic accommodations that occurred throughout the growth of Latin American broadcasting. This domestic dimension and its outcome, the autonomy achieved especially by Latin American television, is important in the context of the political instability and uncertainty of the region and the role played by the media in recent elections (as well as impeachments where television (and radio) industries played important roles in legitimising candidates and winning elections.

As Skidmore (1992) observes in his review of the media in a democratising Latin America, TV is transforming the way political candidates are constructed, marketed, and consolidated. It is also transforming the way politicians govern once they reach office. This book shows the domestic policies and international relations that over the course of the twentieth century made it possible for Latin American broadcasting industries to achieve this position of political strength and autonomy. It might also point the way to an understanding of similar process occurring today in other countries such as those of eastern Europe.

Country studies

Mexico and Brazil now have two of the largest media monopolies in the world: Televisa and TV Globo. These giants, both with significant transnational operations, are rooted in the practically monopolistic control of their enormous domestic markets. The Televisa and Globo empires, basically controlled by individuals and their families rather than by corporations, encompass all aspects of production and distribution of television, radio, film, video, and much of publishing in their respective countries. They have sizable export industries and foreign media holdings, including, in the case of Televisa part ownership of PanAmSat, one of the world's largest private satellite companies, and the largest Hispanic TV network in the United States. They are king-makers in their countries, wielding enormous political power in the selection and even legitimisation of national leaders.

Venezuela follows the Mexican and Brazilian model of a strong domestic media monopoly, integrating all aspects of the industry and wielding enormous independent political power. In Venezuela two large family-owned companies dominate the market rather than the single monopolies of Mexico and Brazil, probably because Venezuelan broadcasting developed under democratically elected governments in a two-party system rather than under one-party or authoritarian rule, as was the case in Mexico and Brazil.

Peru, Colombia, and Argentina have more fragmented broadcasting industries, all three of which are in transition towards increased private control, greater monopolisation, and growing political influence. Peru's fragmentation was the result of the broadcasting's initial failure to reach an accommodation with the state under the military, and, later, to weaknesses within the Peruvian state and political system. Colombia's historical fragmentation was the result of a balance of power between the two ruling parties and their agreement to keep broadcasting under state control as a guarantor of equality of access by the two parties to broadcasting's assets and power. In Argentina broadcasting's fragmentation was the result first of Juan Peron's and later the military's control of television and the reluctance (and often inability) of broadcasters to identify closely with domestic political forces in a highly unstable environment. Uruguay and Chile, emerging from authoritarian control of the media, are redefining state-media relations in the direction of privatisation and deregulation under elected governments. Broadcasting in the two countries is in transition and will probably remain fragmented as a result of new foreign actors and strong domestic competition in local markets.

Each country has a history of media policies and debates, marked by confrontations among economic and political forces concerning the organisation of the media and the distribution of their benefits in society. There are significant internal geographic, social, and political differences in the region. Yet, there are commonalities and influences that are shared by all Latin American countries. The strong presence of the US Government and media industries during the early years of broadcasting in Latin America and at strategic moments for the US Government (World War II) and the networks (limitations on the national market) are two such commonalities. The ability of Latin American domestic broadcasting industries, having achieved a certain size, autonomy, and internationalisation, to adopt to changing contexts and reach analogous accommodations with domestic political power seems to account for other similarities of outcome within the different national contexts.

The present similarities in Latin American broadcasting make it important to identify the paths by which each nation reached the present state of development of their domestic broadcasting industries. The alternative is to say that the development of a strong, private, largely unregulated, and politically autonomous broadcasting industry was unavoidable. This is the argument of those who see the influence of international relations as all powerful in setting the course of Latin American broadcasting. It is, however, an argument that flies in the face of what occurred in other regions of the world, including the United States, Europe, and much of Asia and Africa, where vastly different broadcasting institutions emerged, for the most part in a largely similar international context.

To a large extent an argument of inevitability rules out any possibility of change. If how broadcasting developed in Latin America was unavoidable as a result of dependency or of some other form of insertion in the world, then achieving future, more democratic media structures with the greater participation of civil society is impossible without international reform. What I attempt to illustrate is that change is possible when domestic actors are able to reach a different set of accommodations, even within a powerful and ever changing international context.

Latin American broadcasting is not an atavistic product of poverty, underdevelopment, or tyranny, nor is it an exclusive product of US imperialism. Foreign influence was exerted strategically, randomly, and pervasively over many decades. Yet, more than the product of their foreign relations, Latin American broadcasting industries are the product of a complex interplay of strong and weak domestic governments and markets, authoritarian and populist policies, and largely excluded social forces. The possibility of changing domestic media structures continues to exist within the societies of Latin America, although, as in the past, foreign relations remain a part of the equation for change.

1 *The international relations of Latin American broadcasting*

H istorically, international relations have been seen as one, if not the main, explanation for how Latin American broadcasting evolved. The reasons supporting this explanation, however, differ. They are based on one or a combination of different theories or 'views' of how international relations work. One theory, shared by many Latin American scholars and Marxist intellectuals in other regions, is a Marxist-inspired dependency framework according to which the development of Latin American broadcasting was mainly the result of the dependent economic relations of the region. According to another theory, derived from a realist framework, the international relations of Latin American broadcasting are the outcome of state-inspired actions, mainly from the United States. A third view or theory, more in line with liberalism, sees the development of commercial broadcasting in Latin America as the logical outcome of the free flow of ideas and of the evolution of communication technology. Whatever theory is used to explain foreign influence, there is little question that the foreign presence in the Latin American media, and especially in broadcasting, has been strong. What is less clear is how determinant a role foreign influence played in the formation of Latin American broadcasting as we know it today. This chapter explores this influence in the region.

About 25 years ago the foreign content and control of radio waves, television screens, newspapers columns, advertising copy, and magazines racks became a matter of heated domestic debate and policy initiatives throughout Latin America. Philosophers, sociologists, semiologists, political scientists, and politicians spoke out against the United States' domination and control of the region's media resources.[1] By 1970 the US television networks had direct investments in most Latin American television channels (Table 1), and US films and TV series accounted for the majority of the imported content of Latin America's television screens,

---

1 In 1967 Venezuelan philosopher Antonio Pasquali (1967) published a scathing attack on television and its 'Americanised' content. The same year journalist and politician Eleazer Diaz Rangel (1967) condemned the Latin American press' dependence on US news agencies, and Marta Colomina de Rivera (1968) denounced the pernicious effect of US TV programmes on women and children. Brazilians raised their voices against the new Americanised 'mass' media (Cohen 1971), (Muniz Sodre 1971), (Miceli 1972), and Armand Mattelart and Ariel Dorfman (1970), working at the University of Chile, published their widely read analysis of US comic books, *How to Read Donald Duck: Mass Communication and Colonialism.*

of which there was considerable (Table 2). In most countries advertising by US companies, prepared by US agencies, led the lists of Latin America's largest national advertisers. US wire services Associated Press and the United Press International supplied between 60 and 83 per cent of the international news, including news about other Latin American countries, in almost all the newspapers in the region (CIESPAL 1967, Kaplun 1973, Varis 1985).

Table 1 – US Investments in Latin American TV Channels

Network	Country	Channels
ABC	Argentina	Channel 11
	Chile	Channels 13 and 4
	Colombia	Channel 9
	Costa Rica	Channel 7
	Dominican Republic	Channel 7
	Ecuador	Channel 7, 6, and 3
	El Salvador	Channels 2 and 4
	Guatemala	Channel 3
	Honduras	Channel 5
	Panama	Channel 2
	Uruguay	Channel 12
	Venezuela	Channel 4
NBC	Argentina	Channel 9
	Peru	Channel 9
	Venezuela	Channel 2
CBS	Argentina	Channel 13
	Peru	Channel 13
	Venezuela	Channel 8
Time-Life	Argentina	PROARTEL Channel 13
	Brazil	TV Globo
	Venezuela	Channel 8

Source: Luís Ramiro Beltrán and Elizabeth Fox, *Comunicación dominada: los Estados Unidos en los medios de America Latina*. Mexico: Nueva Imagen, 1980.

Table 2 – Imported Television Programmes on Latin American TV

Country	1973 (%)	1983 (%)
Argentina	10	49
Brazil	n/a	30
Chile	55	n/a
Colombia	34	n/a
Cuba	n/a	24
Dominican Rep.	50	n/a
Ecuador	n/a	66
Guatemala	84	n/a
Mexico	39	34
Uruguay	62	n/a
Venezuela	n/a	38

n/a= data not available

Source: Tapio Varis, *International Flow of Television Programs*, Paris: UNESCO, 1985

Many Latin American scholars applied a Marxist-inspired dependency framework to explain the role of foreign influence on the development of domestic broadcasting media. According to this framework, the economic backwardness of Latin America was the result of historical, structural forces in the region's development and its international relations (Cardoso and Faletto 1979, vii). The region's 'cultural' dependency was the result of these same forces. A system was dependent from the economic point of view when the accumulation and expansion of capital could not find its essential dynamic component within the system. The 'cultural dependency' of the Latin American media was the logical outgrowth of foreign economic influence in the region, mainly from the United States. Cultural dependency was manifest in the commercial nature and foreign content of Latin American broadcasting.

Although dependency theory was used by many scholars from the region to explain the international relations, as well as the domestic policies of Latin American broadcasting, other explanations look beyond economic relations. Realist theory, by focusing on the state as the main actor in international relations, can be used to explain many applications of the media in international relations. For example,

(1) The direct state control of foreign broadcasting systems such as the French government's extension of its radio and television services into both private and public broadcasting systems of Francophone African countries.

(2) State-run broadcasting international programmes for political aims, for example, BBC, RFI, VOA, Radio Moscow, Radio Marti and Radio Free Europe, and the international shortwave and satellite broadcasting activities of China and Iran.

(3) Government activities employed in war and peacetime to influence the media systems of foreign countries such as direct funding for lobbying to influence legislation on the media, training of foreign journalists and technicians, provision and subsidies to foreign media, including capital and materials like newsprint and raw film.

According to realist theory, a state uses its broadcasting and other resources internationally to influence foreign media content, determine the broadcasting institutions another country develops, and define what information a foreign public receives. The motivation for these activities is political rather than economic. In wartime, state actions include international media appeals to weaken the support of the inhabitants of an enemy state for its leaders, actions or policies. In times of peace or cold war, broadcasting like surrogate radios appeal directly to the foreign individual or group, by-passing the state and thereby undercutting the foreign state's public support for an issue, enhancing the image of the 'sender' society, and encouraging internal political change. State-supported international broadcasting activities can have economic repercussions, but their primary motivation is political.

Some examples of the international relations of Latin American broadcasting that fit within a realist framework include the US Government's subsidy for the expansion of the Hollywood and Mexican film industries in Latin America during the Second World War; the US government's funding of Chilean opposition paper *El Mercurio* during the Allende administration in Chile; US government opposition to the New World Information and Communication Order and eventual withdrawal from UNESCO; and today, US Government shortwave and television broadcasting into Cuba. In each case the media are employed as strategic instruments of international relations to further political goals and the national interest and not primarily for economic gain.

Realist theory, with its emphasis on the state as the dominant actor, provides important insights into the international relations of broadcasting. For example:

(1) *A tendency to see the media in international relations as state rather than industry dominated*, 'The *US*'s control of the world media ... Japan's attack on the US media industries ... France's push into African television.

(2) *A tendency to support an ideal of a national culture as a defence against the cultural onslaught of other states.* Much of the thinking in the movement for national communication policies and the New World Information and Communication Order was state-oriented. State policies for cultural imports and national quotas on foreign ownership and content of the media are realist, state-oriented tools for national survival and the defence of national culture in a 'hostile' world.

(3) *The 'offensive' use by states of broadcasting as a means of struggle in international relations*: radio wars, support for opposition radio stations to undermine a hostile state, state-led international policy initiatives in the distribution of radio spectrum resources, and the debate over international cultural policies through organisations like UNESCO and the United Nations.

From disinformation campaigns to interference in the types of media institutions another state develops, the use of the media as a tool of international relations, as separate from military or economic force, falls within realist theory. To the extent that one state attempts to control the communication media of another state – what its people see, hear, think, and want, and how they organise their communication resources – realist theories offer insights into the role of broadcasting in international relations.

Other theories that look beyond the economic or state relations of international communications include liberalism. Liberalism applied to communication and broadcasting embraces the rights of free speech and the free flow of information as a way to maximise the general welfare, insure the efficient operation of the market, and guarantee democracy and the marketplace of ideas. If state and economic interests have dominated much of the exercise of international broadcasting, liberalism has been the dominant image and justification for its operation. Much of the exercise of political and economic power in the last century has been carried out in the name of the free flow of ideas, goods, and services. Liberals have argued the importance of free speech and a free press for the development of liberal democracies, and the need to emancipate the media from state control and regulation.[2]

Technological change and economic growth have fostered liberal theories, according to which the media have been rendered 'stateless' by the inability of states

---

2 In the aftermath of the Second World War, for example, the US State Department and various journalistic organisations joined forces in an attempt to attach statements guaranteeing American-style freedom of the press to certain peace treaties and to the United Nations agreements. These attempts are documented in Blanchard, 1986. Other liberal theorists have urged expanding the scope of the first amendment internationally to cover all forms of electronic media. Ithiel de Sola Pool, proponent of liberalism, for example, states: 'The onus is on us to determine whether free societies in the twenty-first century will conduct electronic communication under the conditions of freedom established for the domain of print through centuries of struggle, or whether that great achievement will become lost in a confusion about new technologies' (1983, 10).

to control the flow of information and entertainment across their national borders. Changes in communication and transportation have produced the potential for large-scale cultural, political, and economic exchange among previously separate people. These 'globalist' liberal theories see the relations among states embedded in and fundamentally governed by a larger set of processes of exchange of goods and ideas and of technological advancement. Industrial modernism falls within this strain of liberalism that sees in the rapid flow of vastly increased amounts of information a way to reduce the control of the state and empower civil society.

Liberal theories of international communications have been aided by republican liberalism's support for the universal desirability of democracy and the rights of free speech. Article 19 of The Universal Declaration of Human Rights was adopted by the United Nations in 1948.[3] Much of the post-war struggle over the distribution of ideas and information in the world has been centred around the implementation of this right. It has been interpreted, mainly by those who control the majority of the resources of information and entertainment, as the right to exercise this control freely without protective tariffs on cultural imports, government control of news flow, or national policies limiting direct broadcast satellites or transborder information and data flow.

In contrast to realism and liberalism, theories derived from Marxist analysis like cultural imperialism and dependency have focused on the material base of the international expansion of media industries. According to these theories, cultural dependency is the logical result of foreign economic dependence and influence. Latin American dependency analysis emerged from the crisis of development,[4] including import substitution, and the conviction that dependency was a key explanatory element for the region's economic woes and inability to prosper. For these theories, underdevelopment was not a rudimentary phase of development or a result of traditional attitudes and cultures, as development theorists would maintain, but the form in which these economies were inserted in world markets. The Latin American theories of dependency reconceptualised imperialism from the perspective of the periphery. In the area of communication and culture, dependency was expressed in terms of cultural domination. Oppressed cultures were suffocated by the cultures of their masters, at times with the assistance of 'national facilitators.' Dependency analysis provided insights into the complex set of associations within which the external dimensions were determinative in varying degrees and internal variables reinforced the pattern of external linkages (Valenzuela and Valenzuela 1978).

World systems analysis added other dimension to Marxist dependency theory. James Schwoch (1990), for example, used a world systems approach to analyse the US influence on the Latin American radio industry between 1890 and 1939. While viewing the development of radio broadcasting as a key element in US economic

---

3 This article states: 'Everyone has the right to freedom of opinion and expression, this right includes freedom to hold opinions without interference and to seek, receive and impart information and ideas through any media and regardless of frontiers.'

4 Modernisation theories focused on development as an endogenous process. Underdevelopment was the result of traditional attitudes and cultural practices that could be modified by the diffusion of modern attitudes via the educational system and the mass media. Import substitution was based on the idea that national economies were capable of industrialisation by means of state support for endogenous production. States would replace externally with internally oriented development, supported by a relatively autonomous national market.

expansion, Schwoch saw the global rise of broadcasting as a manifestation of the long history of capitalism. The terms of the debate – private enterprise versus state-ownership and the primacy of new technology in modernisation versus traditional practices and technologies – were defined through US government and industry participation in international communications conferences that structured the international decision-making process concerning the electromagnetic spectrum.

Schwoch sees the evolution of the US radio industry in Latin America from selling equipment to selling programming and advertising as steps in a larger social, political, economic, and cultural process – the establishment of a mass broadcasting and consumer culture. He concludes that international capital in the radio industry was eventually able to provide a semblance of order and coordination along its own lines of rationality, 'Although international capitalists at the centre of the radio industry did not always provide the initial vision for radio's economic well-being, they did always see their work as a global rather than a merely domestic activity' (140). According to Marxist theories, including imperialism, dependency, and world systems, the investments of the US distributors and broadcasters in Latin America and the role of the US Government in supporting their overseas operations were the determinant factor in the evolution of Latin American broadcasting.

The combination of realist politics, liberal rhetoric, and Marxist economic interest was key in the international expansion of commercial broadcasting industries. Realism, liberalism, and Marxism, however, although insightful in terms of providing motivations for foreign influence, provide little explanation for understanding the institutions through which this influence is mediated and received by the acquiring society and culture. Realist, liberal and Marxist theories alike are largely unable to consider plurality, differences, and conflicts within receiving (or sending) societies. Often applied mechanically, these views of the international relations of Latin American broadcasting often result in a one-dimensional and instrumental view of broadcasting industries that obscures the complexity of their exercise and the contradictions in their interior. In other word, these theories, by focusing on the motives and actions of the foreign state or industry, play down or ignore the conflicts and accommodations that occur at the domestic level among different economic and political actors.

Some theorists, building on Marxism and dependency analyses, have attempted to integrate in the study of international communications some of the elements ignored by realists' and Marxists' 'flat' view of national culture. Studies of modernity, for example, place the question of cultural domination or imperialism within the broader framework of the spread of modernity with all it represents of harm and benefit to the receiving society.[5] Latin American theorists working in the field of communication and culture have examined the processes of mediation and the

---

5 Tomlinson (1991) places the locus of modernity's cultural imposition not in the content of the media themselves but in the simultaneous export of technology and capitalist enterprise (economic imperialism) and the export of the West's social imaginary signification of development. Cultural imperialism can therefore be said to appear in the plane of the imaginary. So, though cultural contacts with Western modernity may inevitably result in the decay of traditional worldviews and practices, this does not necessarily mean that these have to be replaced with the (impoverished) cultural narratives of the West. Tomlinson locates the of cultural dependency in the realm of the social imaginary and the institutional frameworks that give it form:

> So far as non-Western societies have been institutionally subordinate to Western ones, so have their culturally self-formative capacities. This is not a subordination of human imagination as such, but of the institutions that contextualise and constrain it ... and the praxis which brought about the institutions of modernity was, of course, a Western praxis (162).

formation of hybrids that occur in the interaction of foreign and domestic cultures (Canclini 1982; Martin Barbero, 1987). The work of these authors provides important insights into what occurs on the level of the community or individual in the process of cultural confrontation and interaction. It does not address the impact of the interaction of foreign and domestic cultures on the formation of domestic broadcasting industries.

The domestic forces that helped form broadcasting in eight Latin American countries are examined in the chapters that follow. The following broad overview of the international relations of Latin American broadcasting systems explores the combination of different forces within the United States that occurred over the course of the development of Latin American broadcasting. This combination involved the evolving relationship between the US Government and the US domestic broadcasting industry and how it affected their international relations.

The international relations of Latin American broadcasting

The United States has been the main actor in the international relations of Latin American broadcasting. Historically, the principal motive of the United States Government in its relations with Latin American broadcasting has been to support US commercial interests and counter the threat of the control of broadcasting by a hostile foreign state or domestic political power. These actions are understandable in a realist framework. In the first case the foreign power was Nazi Germany. In the second case it was communism or the threat of what were perceived as the creeping socialist tendencies of state-directed economies in Latin America.

Except during the Second World War, US Government influence in Latin America was for the most part exercised through the US private media industries. These industries were strong enough domestically to prevent the US Government from taking a protagonist position in international broadcasting. US Government and private industry worked in tandem in Latin America to promote private ownership of the media and the free flow of information, insure politically docile domestic media, and safeguard US interests. By working through the private commercial media throughout the hemisphere, the combined actions of the US Government and private broadcasting industry helped contribute to the ultimate political strength and 'autonomy' of Latin American broadcasters. The international relations of Latin American broadcasting played a key role in setting these processes in motion and, in some cases, influencing the turning points of domestic relationships. Specifically:

(1) The initial impact of foreign capital, technology and creative talent on domestic radio industries.

(2) The impact of state-directed efforts by the US Government, often exercised through the private US media, to insure support for the Allied cause during the Second World War, and, later, a similar effort to combat the spread of what were perceived as communist-inspired ideologies.

(3) The opposition by the US private broadcasters and Government to the

efforts of populist/redistributive states to bring broadcasting industries under national policy guidelines.

The initial impact of foreign capital, technology and creative talent on domestic radio industries

As the small experimental radio stations of every country of Latin America grew, they inevitably came into contact with domestic and international forces, not the least of which were the US commercial radio networks, advertising agencies, and equipment manufacturers eager to invest in Latin America and develop markets for their products. In the 1920s Mexico was second only to Canada in the volume of American radio equipment it imported; Mexican annual imports of equipment topped $250,000 in 1925 and surpassed $1 million in 1929 (Schwoch 1990, 107) In many smaller Latin American countries, without protective tariffs or state subsidies, domestic radio artists, producers, advertisers, and station owners were unable to compete with cheaper imports from larger countries of the region or from the United States. Foreign capital and recorded music and programmes flowed into the Latin American radio stations in the 1920s and 1930s.

The US Government took an active role in supporting the expansion of the US commercial media in Latin America. Schwoch's study of the radio industry in the region between 1900 and 1939 documents activities of the US consuls in Brazil in the promotion of exports and sales of American radio equipment in that country and in the establishment of the private, commercial American-style broadcasting model. This included programming, advertising, training and workshops for Brazilian technicians, American music made available in sheet music and recordings, radio fairs, and exhibits. Schwoch (1990,106) concludes:

> The American Government, as represented by consuls and attaches: and the American radio industry, as represented by manufactures, exporters, salesmen, and traders, protected and promoted the growth of the American radio industry and American-style broadcasting throughout Latin America.

US manufactures of radio receivers and equipment were among the first actors in the formation of the Latin American broadcasting industries. One of the most powerful radio stations in Buenos Aires, Radio Sud America, was operated by a branch of RCA, originally established to sell RCA equipment. In Uruguay, both General Electric and Westinghouse had associations with stations in Montevideo (Schwoch, 110-1). The Columbian Broadcasting System, CBS, set up the Cadena de las Americas, and the National Broadcasting Company, NBC, operated the Cadena Panamericana with affiliated radio stations in most countries of the region (Diehl 1977). Other foreign companies, more interested in using radio to sell their products than in the growth of the technology, also entered Latin American radio broadcasting. Sydney Ross pharmaceutical company, for example, established one of the earliest radio networks in Colombia; in Chile three US mining companies operated their own commercial radio network.[6] Between 1920 and 1930, US companies (and broadcasters), notably the US radio networks and radio manufacturers, invested in radio station and radio equipment distributors throughout the hemisphere, many times forming partnerships with local enterprises.

The impact of state-directed efforts by the US Government

Although the nascent US private broadcasting industry moved rapidly to invest in Latin American radio industries initially, the US government was not far behind in its efforts to broadcast directly to the region.[7] In fact, as early as 1924, during the administration of President Calvin Coolidge, the US began shortwave broadcasts to Latin America, transmitting over commercial radio station WRC in Washington, D.C. This was a result of efforts by the Pan American Union, located in Washington, D.C., to secure the location of shortwave frequencies to enable it to transmit programmes of Pan American music to Latin America. Programmes were either devoted exclusively to a single country, including music and a short address by the country's diplomatic representative, or composed of music from several countries with an address of a general nature. In 1927, the Department of the Navy agreed to broadcast the Union's programme on long wave transmitters from its stations NAA in Arlington, Virginia.

According to the official history of the early US Government radio operation (Gregory, 1970), in 1929, numerous requests from Latin American governments asking that these programmes be transmitted throughout the hemisphere led the Director General of the Pan American Union, Leo S. Rowe, to inform Secretary of State Frank B. Kellogg that he was convinced that the best plan was for the Navy to broadcast the programmes simultaneously on the standard and shortwave frequencies. On 2 March, 1929, President Coolidge signed Executive Order 5067 assigning the frequencies of 6120 kilocycles and 9550 kilocycles for use by Station NAA of the Navy Department for the specific purpose of broadcasting programmes arranged by the Pan American Union.

Little use was made of these frequencies, however, because the new administration of President Herbert Hoover made no attempt to implement the Union's proposal for utilising the radio frequencies. The Navy, either unable or unwilling to do so, did not provide the necessary equipment, and efforts by the Pan American Union to acquire the transmitters through other sources were unsuccessful. Three additional frequencies, however, were allocated to the Navy for use by the Pan American Union. These frequencies, like the earlier ones, were not used, bringing

---

6 The contrast between how radio developed in Canada and in the United States provides a good example of the international influence of US radio industry in the 1920s and 1930s. The Canadian radio industry started out much like the industry in the United States, almost exclusively privately owned. In the early 1930s, however, the Canadian parliament appointed a Commission of Radio Broadcasting, which issued a report in 1932 recommending a drift towards government ownership and operation of stations, limiting advertising to 5 per cent of programme time. The motivation behind this measure was not strictly a loathing of commercialism, it was a belief that commercialism brought dominance of programming by the United States. The members of the commission believed that the majority of programmes being heard in Canada came from sources outside the country and this reception would tend 'to mold the minds of the young people in the home to ideas and opinions that are not Canadian.' The main emphasis behind the founding of the Canadian Broadcasting System as a government-subsidised entity was the strongly held belief that only government ownership could secure Canadian programming in the face of the powerful commercial radio industry in the United States (G. Douglas 1987, 84).

7 Much of the information in this section is based on Bruce N. Gregory, *The Broadcasting Service: An Administrative History*, The United States Information Agency Special Monograph Series, No. 1, Washington: USIA, 1970, USIA Historical Collection. Citations of documents and correspondence are taken from citations contained in this document.

Gregory to speculate that a circumstantial case could be made that the frequencies were assigned primarily as part of a general effort by the United States to reserve for itself as much of the high frequency spectrum as it could. The Navy's attitude was expressed by Captain S.C. Hooper, Director of Naval Communications.[8] The United States, it appeared, was content to limit its official international broadcasting activities merely to the strategic 'reservation' of shortwave frequencies.

Shortwave broadcasting, however, was revolutionising the conduct of foreign policy throughout the world: Radio Moscow began in 1929, the French in 1931, the BBC in 1932, and Germany in 1933. 'The capability of states to penetrate territorial frontiers at will via radio, and thereby directly influence foreign public opinion, significantly altered the international environment of the new administration of President Franklin Roosevelt (Gregory 1970, 1-9). For the first time, these events forced the US Government to adopt a position on the use of broadcasting as an instrument of foreign policy, It led ultimately, in the spring of 1934, to a Government proposal supporting the establishment of a government-owned-and-operated radio station (Gregory 1970, 1-10).

Sectors within the Roosevelt administration as well as commercial broadcasters, however, opposed this measure. Even before the bill authorising funding for the station was sent to Congress, a representative of the American Telephone and Telegraph Company had informed the State Department that the company 'would be glad to cooperate in any way possible ... in the development of the very best means of communication with the Latin American countries' (Gregory 1970, 1-28). The United States Information Agency, USIA, History concludes that the interest expressed by the commercial broadcasters was the result of a fundamental assumption on their part that their independence would be threatened by the entrance of the US Government into the field of radio broadcasting, and that the opposition from commercial broadcasters was a factor in the bill's demise (Gregory 1970, 1-29).

In 1935, the Pan American Union provided another stimulus for the US Government to reconsider the issue of international broadcasting in Latin America. In November the Union convened an informal meeting of representatives of the Navy, the Federal Communication Commission, FCC, and the State Department to consider the ways and means of financing a Pan American radio station. (Gregory 1970, 1-33) The funding of the station was the main obstacle to reaching an agreement. 'Whatever the reason,' Gregory observes, 'President Roosevelt chose not to act on the Department of State's recommendation [to fund the station] and, without his prestige and full support behind it, the innovation of public international broadcasting was impossible at this time' (1-45).

The history reports that beginning in 1937 the failure of the Executive Branch to reach a decision on government-supported international broadcasting led to a shift in initiative from the State Department to Congress – a change that was marked by the introduction of several bills calling for the establishment of a government-owned broadcasting station for Latin America (Gregory 1970, 2-1). The

---

8 'The power and strength of sovereign nations, Captain Hooper observed, depends and has depended since the beginning of time on initiative, brains, and ability to beat the other fellow to it. Now, if the United States can get 230 frequencies occupied prior to other nations, why should not we keep them? ... the longer the United States delays in putting its high-frequency circuits on the map internationally, the larger will be the proportion of stations occupied by foreign nations' (Gregory 1970, 1-5).

increased public visibility of the debate as a result of congressional interest made it necessary for the President to take a decision. The result was a series of interim measures which 'while they did not close the door to a publicly owned broadcasting service, *had the effect of expanding the use of privately owned facilities as a means of achieving the foreign policy objectives envisaged by the proponents of a government-owned-and-operated radio station*' (Gregory 1970, 2-2) (emphasis added).

Gregory observes that although President Roosevelt personally favoured a government-owned-and-operated shortwave radio station, he gave only limited support to a congressional bill to provide funding and organisation for this initiative [the Celler bill], 'presumably because of his awareness of the political risks involved.' The bill evoked the vigorous public opposition of the US private broadcasting industry, 'a political fact that both the Administration and Congress were to balance against the perceived need for an official counter to Axis radio propaganda in Latin America' (2-17).

The growth of private shortwave broadcasting to Latin America

NBC was the first private commercial broadcaster to provide shortwave services to Latin America. By 1934 it was transmitting programmes via shortwave for direct international consumption as well as to Latin American radio stations for re-broadcast. Four years later NBC had established an international division to deal exclusively with programme creation and production in six languages including Spanish and Portuguese. Boyd, (1974, 41) in his 'pre-history' of the Voice of America states that NBC felt, as did other broadcasters, that the US Government might erect its own station and therefore wanted to be able to argue that private broadcasters were providing adequate service to Latin America. CBS, like NBC, Boyd observes, also saw the commercial possibilities of shortwave programming and wanted to help provide a service which would discourage the US Government from entering the field.[9] In 1937 the Columbia Broadcasting System established a small separate shortwave programmes bureau and began regular international broadcasting to Europe and Latin America.

Commercials were not permitted on the shortwave broadcasts of the US companies until 1939 when the FCC lifted their classification as experimental stations. The first commercial programme was sponsored on NBC by the United Fruit Company. By the early 1940s, Crosley, another commercial shortwave company, had organised Cadena Radio Interamericana with 15 stations, mostly in Central America (Boyd 1974, 42). In 1940, CBS President William S. Paley made a trip to Latin America to promote the idea of a Latin American network. He returned with contracts from 64 stations, all of whom agreed to carry a minimum of one hour of programming per day. (Boyd, 43) Three other commercial companies – General Electric, Westinghouse, and the Crosley Corporation – also undertook regular international broadcasting to Latin America. The commercial

---

9 The World Wide Broadcasting Corporation was the only international station which was not operated by an electrical manufacturer or domestic broadcaster. The station was founded in 1927 by Walter Lemmon, who has been President Wilson's radio officer at the Versailles Peace Conference. The station was financed by contribution from various philanthropists including IBM president Thomas J. Watson and later the Rockefeller Foundations.

networks felt the entrance of the US Government in the field of international broadcasting would 'unnecessarily duplicate existing private stations and would constitute an entering wedge for public control and operation of all domestic broadcasting in the United States' (Gregory, 2-22),

The US Government's accommodation with the private sector

In 1938 the US Government finally came to a decision on what to do with its international shortwave frequencies to Latin America. Four of the five US Government shortwave frequencies were assigned to the private sector, two to World Wide Broadcasting and two to General Electric. With the one frequency on loan to CBS, all five Pan American frequencies were now in the hands of private broadcasters. Gregory observes, 'Not only would it be difficult to secure return of the frequencies at some future time, the broadcasters had already demonstrated that even on the relatively marginal issue of frequency assignments they had the power and will to successfully oppose the [State] Department's wishes. The moral was clear. If the Department was unwilling to confront the broadcasters publicly on the frequency question, it would be even less likely to be willing to do so on the larger and more emotional issue of a government station for international broadcasting (Gregory, 2-37).

Two bills [Chavez and Celler] introduced in Congress in 1938 to set up a government shortwave stations to Latin America were strongly opposed by the private broadcasters invited to present their views in hearings. The case against government broadcasting was most forcefully stated by Mark Ethridge, President of the National Association of Broadcasters. Ethridge argued:

> It is desirable for the United States to impress its culture on Latin America by indirection and to further the Good Neighbour policy by projecting a living pattern of our democracy, presenting the best of our music, institutions, traditions of liberty and freedom ... programmes of entertainment ... and the news of the day, uncoloured and uncensored. While this can be done by government ... under the existing system of broadcasting in the United States it can be better and more effectively accomplished by private entrepreneurs. (cited in Gregory, 2-59)

Ethridge drew the comparison between the possible US Government control of media for the dissemination of news and information in Latin America and the authoritarian states in Europe where government control and operation of radio, news, newspapers and other instruments of communicating information was already a fait accompli. 'It [US Government broadcasting] suggests the Nazi philosophy which seeks to fuse the people with a common thought, with common aims, and ultimately obtains complete submission to the thinking of a small group.' (Cited by Boyd 1974, 44).

Not until America's entry into the Second World War did the US Government become directly involved in broadcasting in Latin America. Compelled by the exigencies of war, the United States Government undertook international broadcasting on a massive scale. By that time, however, the model and philosophy of ing on a massive scale. By that time, however, the model and philosophy of commercial broadcasting was firmly established both in Latin America and in terms of the route through which the US Government would broadcast to the region and the world.

The impact of the Second World War on Latin American broadcasting

The rearming of Germany during the 1930s and its increasing trade with Latin America, and the emigration of German nationals to the region, as well as the state-directed and subsidised broadcasting and cultural activities of the German Government in Latin American countries,[10] put a different spin on how the US Government perceived the role of culture and communication and especially broadcasting to Latin America. The growth of the Pan-American Movement to unify the American hemisphere on a multilateral basis started in the United States in the 1930s. The move was formalised in the Eighth Inter-American Conference in Lima in 1938, and after the outbreak of war in 1939, with the establishment within the US Government of the Inter-American Financial and Economic Advisory Committee, and, in June 1940, the Inter-American Development Commission. The importance of the strategic relationship between Latin America and the United States at the start of the war is described in the *History of the Office of the Coordinator of Inter-American Affairs*, a historical report on the war administration, published by the United Sates Government Printing Office (Washington, 1947), hereafter referred to as *History*.

> ... in the United States, with a powerful defensive military machine now an evident need, it was realised that many strategic materials could no longer be obtained from areas now under control of the Axis powers. For these reasons, persons in the United States became interested in easing the situation in Latin America by large purchases of raw materials, thereby supplying foreign exchange which in turn could be used to purchase needed manufactured and semi-fabricated goods and which would thus afford revenues to the governments of the other American republics through import and export duties. These activities would not only relieve financial pressures but also would maintain employment at a level which would tend to prevent discontent and disorder and thus eliminate a fertile field for Nazi propaganda (*History*, 4).

Nelson Rockefeller, the second son of John D. Rockefeller II was the main actor behind the establishment of the Office of Coordinator of Inter-American Affairs, set up to manage strategic relations with the region. In August 1940 Rockefeller was named Coordinator of the Office for Commercial and Cultural Relations between the American Republics, subordinate to the Council of National Defence. The Coordinator's objective was to:

---

10 These cultural activities included German schools, cultural centres, athletic clubs, and other societies, subsidised press agencies, Axis controlled radio stations, and German-produced motion pictures.

... establish and maintain liaison between the Advisory Commission of the Council of National Defence, the several departments and establishments of the Government and such other agencies, public or private, as he might deem necessary or desirable, to insure proper coordination of, with economy and efficiency, the activities of the Government with respect to Hemisphere defence, with particular reference to the commercial and cultural aspects of the problem (*History*, 7).

The coordinator was directly responsible to the President, in cooperation with the Department of State, for a programme for the effective use of Government and private facilities in Latin America in the arts and sciences, education, travel, the radio, press, and cinema. The programme's purpose was to further national defence and strengthen the bonds between the nations of the Western Hemisphere. This organisation, launched in August 1940, lasted throughout the war years until May 1946. It changed its name twice (it will be referred to here as CIAA, the Coordinator of Inter-American Affairs), and its personnel grew under the pressure of war until it numbered some 1,100 persons working in the United States and almost 300 technicians abroad. CIAA was instrumental in the formation of some twenty committees of United States citizens in the countries of the region who served to carry out its information activities.

The purpose of the CIAA information programme was two-fold. The first was to inform public opinion in the Americas about 'the significance of the events that are taking place at home and abroad.'[11] The second was to attempt to meet and counteract the propaganda programme of the Axis powers on radio, in news columns and the subsidised press, and through other means of communication.

The Press Division of CIAA furnished news and features to over 1,000 Latin American newspapers, magazines, and radio stations. News was transmitted by shortwave radio, by the direct distribution of feature articles, news photographs, pamphlets and cartoons, and with the publication of a magazine, *En Guardia*. The Radio Division of the CIAA produced its own programmes and worked with private broadcasters, encouraging the NBC and CBS local affiliate chains in Latin America. The Motion Picture Division of the CIAA produced and distributed its own films and cooperated with film companies like Walt Disney Productions to produce and distribute newsreels and films in Latin America. Working with the CIAA, the US motion picture industry refused to sell to any theatre showing Axis films. (Through these efforts, by May 1942, with the exception of two theatres in Buenos Aires, no German films were being shown in Latin America.) Other CIAA programmes worked to maintain the level of advertising by US companies in pro-Allied Latin American media and supply newsprint to friendly publishers.

The *History* reports that when CIAA entered the field in 1940 the situation in regard to radio activities in the Western Hemisphere was not 'particularly promising' (57). Under non-war condition there were 12 shortwave stations broadcasting programmes to the American Republics: CBS (2), Crossly Corporation (1), General Electric Company (3), NBC (2) Western Electric and Manufacturing Company (2), World Wide Broadcasting Foundation (2). Furthermore, it states,

11 US Congress House, Hearings. Second Deficiency Appropriations Bill, 1941, p. 688, cited in *History*, 41.

... little or no profit incentive existed, and the six companies which were in the field commercially were there largely because they hoped at some future time to put their operations on a paying basis. The United States stations were operated with much less power than European-owned radio units, and the [foreign] government-operated stations in London, Berlin, and Rome also had superior equipment (*History*, 58).

As a result of the low transmitting power for Latin America under the control of the US Government and broadcasting industry, the Coordinator's Office found that the only practical way to reach a large audience in the hemisphere was by placing the United States programmes on domestic Latin American commercial stations. The first radio news programme was authorised in April 1941. The broadcasts, compiled by CBS from United States Press Association News, was sent by American Telephone and Telegraph Corporation radio telephone to the Latin American countries. There it was picked up by the International Telephone and Telegraph Company and distributed for broadcasting over a network of domestic long and shortwave stations. Much of the cost of the programme was absorbed by the private US companies involved (*History*, 59).

The accomplishments of the CIAA in radio in the period before the outbreak of war consisted of coordinating and aiding the efforts of the US private shortwave broadcasters transmitting to Latin America. In addition, the Office encouraged NBC and CBS to expand their local affiliates chains in Latin America, with NBC making contracts which resulted in about 125 local affiliated radio stations. CBS contracted with about 74 local stations in the same way. These stations re-broadcast the programmes received from the United States via shortwave from NBC and CBS. The *History* describes the operations of the US Government and private broadcasters in Latin America as follows:

CIAA, working with NBC and CBS produced from the studios of these companies all Spanish and Portuguese language programmes sent out. This plan assisted the two network in maintaining their commercial identities, as a complete Spanish and Portuguese language service was offered by each ... Contracts drawn up by CIAA in connection with shortwave broadcasting covered the use of all transmitting facilities and the actual production of the basic programmes by the broadcasting companies, including the writing of scripts and announcing. They also covered the purchase of station time in the other American republics for re-broadcasting of the more important programmes by station networks associated with NBC and CBS. While CBS and NBC under the contract did the writing of scripts, final authority for all programming rested with CIAA. Regular content directives were issued by the agency on a daily basis, with additional directives for special types of operations (*History*, 63).

CIAA reached radio audiences in Latin America on one of five routes: shortwave broadcasting by stations in the United States; re-broadcasting of shortwave programmes by local stations, regularly followed by the networks affiliated with NBC and CBS; the use of commercial point-to-point delivery of special programmes to local stations for re-broadcasting; sending transcriptions of all type of programmes to local station for their uses; and, the local production of programmes under the direction of the local committees (*History*, 63).[12]

Radio programming included news, prepared by the News Section. (Under the contract with the broadcasting companies, CBS and NBC had the right to adapt scripts supplied by CIAA so long as general directives were followed.[13]) Other programming consisted of feature shows, dramatic presentations, musical programmes, and sports. In addition, many blank records were sent to the coordination committees for local use, as well as all types of necessary electronic equipment (*History*, 65).

In the fall of 1942 the US Government finalised negotiations for leasing back the shortwave broadcasting facilities from the private companies that just a few years earlier had been given the frequencies reserved by the Navy. Under the term of the lease, the broadcaster would continue operating their facilities without profit. In return the Government would pay the cost of the operations. The facilities would be used by the US Government to prepare and transmit programmes, and certain programmes would be produced in collaboration with CBS and NBC staffs. (Pirsein 1979, 28). The companies leasing their facilities to the government were: CBS, Crosley, General Electric, NBC and Westinghouse Radio Stations. Later, World Wide Broadcasting also agreed to the Government's terms.[14]

The Radio Division (with the Motion Picture Division of CIAA) made limited use of a covert subsidiary corporation in its activities in Latin America. A corporation, Prencinradio, a non-profit membership corporation organised under the laws of the State of Delaware, was formed, according to Rockefeller, 'in order to develop and encourage public sympathy with our war objectives on the part of the people of the other American Republics ... through the development of existing media of communication and the creation of new facilities'.[15] Prencinradio's main project in connection with radio was the purchase of a radio company (Sadrep Limitada) in Uruguay for the dissemination of information tending to encourage friendly relations with the United States and to combat Axis propaganda detrimental to the war effort. The radio efforts of Prencinradio, however, were by and large unsuccessful and were discontinued in 1945.

The Radio Division's training programme brought directors of radio stations, radio engineers, and artists to the United States to study techniques and dramatic art. The training programme, carried out in coordination with the major networks

---

12 'By the summer of 1942, local CIAA Coordination Committees were active in radio programme production. For example, the Chile Committee produced two daily news programmes: *Noticiario Mundial-El Mercurio* and *Frente al Conflicto* as well as a weekly *Editorial de la Semana*. Uruguay had a feature programme *Habla America* and a news programme *America Frente a la Guerra*, and the Peruvian Committee sponsored the news programme, *La Escena Mundial*.' (*History*, 24) In Mexico, CIAA project No. 752 consisted of three 10-minute broadcasts six days per week beginning Abril 20 over XEW and XEQ and 44 stations throughout Mexico (cost $175,000 plus $10,000 for one year) (Pirsein 1979, 439).

13 The *History* notes that at first there was some friction over this control, especially with CBS, 'for the company was somewhat concerned over loss of identity in view of its commercial interests in the postwar period, and also because it had a fear that its independence in handling news might be affected' (64).

14 Both NBC and CBS, although under contract with the CIAA for a great deal of Latin American programming, were still programming commercial broadcast to the areas and continued to operate their networks of affiliates and maintain their commercial identity (Pirsein, 34).

15 Nelson A. Rockefeller to Harold D. Smith, 18 June, 1942. *History*, 66.

and independent radio stations, was of particular importance because of the short-age of skilled radio technicians in Latin America at the time.

By the Fall of 1943 CIAA radio activities included: about 200 hours per week of direct short wave broadcasts; local re-broadcasts on about 190 local stations; 100 transcription programmes; and, through 80 local stations, about 230 hours of pro-gramming per week. In addition, through cooperation with US advertisers,[16] another 150 station hours were programmed and directed to Latin America (Pirsein 1979, 37).[17]

The Motion Picture Division of CIAA was mainly concerned with the pro-duction of films by US companies for exhibition in Latin America. Part of its programme was the elimination of Axis newsreels from Latin American theatres. This was carried out through the US film industry, with United States distributors agreeing to withdraw all United States film bookings from theatres that showed objectionable films from enemy powers. The Motion Picture Division made use of the same subsidiary non-profit corporation, Prencinradio, that was used for radio. Insofar as motion pictures were concerned, the programme involved supplying production capital, technical assistance, and equipment for the encouragement of the private film industry in Latin America. The idea was to produce feature films presenting the case for hemisphere solidarity in the war against the Axis. This pro-gramme was justified on the grounds that Latin American films reached a differ-ent audience than United States films and they would be less subject to suspicion of being a part of a United States propaganda campaign.

The first and only motion picture project undertaken by Prencinradio was the stimulation of the Mexican motion picture industry. The objective stated was that production of pictures by the Mexican industry would support the war effort and hemisphere solidarity and would also serve as a means of 'forestalling development of an industry in that country by interests unsympathetic to the United States war effort'.[18] The Prencinradio agreement provided for the sale of US-made motion picture equipment to the two leading motion picture studios in Mexico City, tech-nical training to Mexican technicians, the production of a number of special pro-ject, and cooperation with the Mexican industry in the distribution of films.

---

16 One list of advertisers in a March 1943 'CIAA Advertisers' Cooperation in Latin America Report' includes: Anacin, Bristol Myers, Calox, Colgate, Corn Products, Davis and Lawrence, Dr. D. Jayne, Johnson's Wax, Colymos, Lone Star Cement, Philco, Picot Laboratories, RCA, Scott's Emulsion, Standard Oil, Sterling, Tangee, United Fruit, Vick Chemical, and Zonite (cited in Pirsein, 446).

17 A handbook prepared by the director of the CIAA Communications Division points out a situation where US firms were discovered sponsoring German news programmes on Latin American radio. 'In many of the republics, American advertising budgets are due to the low purchasing potential of the population necessarily small. Some firms could afford to buy time on a station for a news cast broadcast, but could not afford to buy United Press or Association Press news. Neither could the stations afford to buy the high priced American news services. Committed to brqoadcasting news for an American product – without money enoug to buy 'good' news – some of the stations probably found it profitable to use the news they could obatin at no cost from European propaganda sources. Some American advertisers have admitted that they did not know the source of the news they were spon-soring; though they did know it could not be that from American news agencies. To remedy this grotesque situa-tion …' and the report goes on to describe the programme with US advertisers and news agencies. (Francisco, RG 229, Box 43 'Francisco, Don', USIA Historical Collection).

18 Nelson A. Rockefeller to Prencinradio Inc., 27 July, 1942. The Coordinator stated that the programme in Mexico was only the first in a broader plan to develop the motion picture industries in several of the other American Republics (History, 82).

Philosophy of the CIAA

According to official sources (*History*, 166), the objectives of the Communication Division within the CIAA were national defence and the strengthening of hemisphere bonds. The first purpose was to increase technical facilities of communication so as to attain mass coverage in several countries. The second was to add to the amount of material to be communicated and to improve its quality. The third was to utilise these resources for communications to counteract and offset the dissemination of news unfavourable to hemisphere defence, and to develop and spread ideas favourable to the interests of the United States together with those of the other American Republics.[19]

In presenting its budget estimates to Congress and in defending those estimates in appropriation subcommittee hearings, the CIAA emphasised hemisphere defence as the basic reason for its existence. In other words, a realist objective closely coordinated with the operations, goals, and liberal rhetoric of private broadcasters. On January 17, 1941, Rockefeller, testifying before the House Appropriations Committee, voiced the philosophy of the agency as follows:

> The credo on which our entire effort is based is just this: The countries of this hemisphere are composed of free people and free people can and will find the right answers to their defence and salvation – whatever the challenge – if they are given the facts and an opportunity truthfully to understand and appreciate their mutual interest ... We are faced, as we see it, with a very serious aspects of the defence programme. The front line is the aid-to-England programme. The second line of defence is the hemisphere programme. At the present time it is not on a military basis, but we are faced with an economic defence problem and with a psychological defence problem as against propaganda from abroad controlled by Axis groups ... Axis propaganda has swept over the entire hemisphere. *This intellectual imperialism of ideas is at the moment just as serious a threat to the security and defence of the hemisphere as the possibility of a military invasion.*[20] (emphasis added)

In budget hearings for the CIAA, Rockefeller reiterated the importance of hemisphere solidarity to the war. 'It is not only the leaders who must be our confirmed friends. What today is a total war, and unless the people themselves will fight, there will be no real protection against Axis infiltration or invasion. There must be full cooperation between all of the people of the 21 republics of this hemisphere' (*History*, 168).

---

19 In a memorandum of February 28, 1941 to Under Secretary of State Sumner Welles, Mr. Rockefeller indicated the objectives of the Communications Division as: (1) to offset totalitarian propaganda in the other American republics; (2) to remove and correct sources of irritation and misunderstanding arising in this country – as when our motion pictures burlesque Central and South American characters; (3) to emphasise and focus public opinion on the elements making for unity among the Americans; (4) to increase knowledge and understanding of one another's way of life; (5) to give greater expression to the forces of good will between the Americans, in line with the Good Neighbour Policy (*History*, 166).

20 US Congress House, Hearings. *Second Deficiency Appropriations Bill*, 1941, 688, *History*, 167.

Transition to 'Peace' and the Cold War

In addition to their indirect support for the expansion of the US broadcasting industry in Latin America, the activities of the CIAA had a profound effect on the development of the Latin American media. Under government supervision and support, during the war years, the US private broadcasters had seen their initial shortwave and direct radio investments in Latin America expand into a much wider range of media activities. For the first time US news services were widely used in the region, US motion pictures were easily available and without competition, and US radio programming and news, produced by government services and by private broadcasters was aggressively disseminated and used by domestic radio stations. Even the US advertising industry was coordinated in the effort to work with US export to Latin America. After the war, with the exception of the US Government shortwave radio broadcasts, most of the communication and media activities of the CIAA were transferred or returned to the private sector. With the return of peace, for a short time, the private broadcasters produced programmes for the Voice of America on a contract basis. A few years later, the government completely took over VOA activities, and today continues to operate non-commercial shortwave broadcasting and local placement of programming to the audiences and radio stations of Latin America and other countries of the world.

Soon, however, the concerns of the cold war again moved the US government to address the development of broadcasting in Latin America. These concerns, especially after the success of the Cuban Revolution in 1959, were directed against what were seen as state-ownership or control of the media, as in the case of Castro's Cuba, and toward the support for private, commercial, politically conservative mass media industries in the case of most other countries.

During the Cold War and especially during the Economic Recovery Plan, Europe was the US government's first priority in terms of communication and culture.[21] Concern by the US Government over the impact of exposure to US media in Latin America and for the attitudes towards communism of populations in that region, however, paralleled these European concerns. A study carried out for USIA in urban Chile in 1953, for example, specifically addressed the relationship between attitudes towards communism and exposure to US media. The findings were favourable to international expansion of the US media. The study found that except in Santiago, Chileans exposed to US media were more likely than those not exposed to believe that communism brought no special benefit to the workers of the country.[22]

A study carried out in the ten largest Brazilian cities by the United States Information Services of the American Embassy in Rio de Janeiro in 1956

---

21 This need is argued by Charles.D. Jackson, a top officer under General Robert A. McClure in the Anglo-American Psycho-logical Warfare Division of Eisenhower's Headquarters Staff (SHAEF) in (Jackson, 1951, 328).

> ... in the cold war of words all our deeds abroad, all our writings, all our publications, all our expressions of thought must be weighed according to their propaganda impact. That is why all private activities affecting public opinion abroad have, in effect, a propaganda aspect, using the word without an invidious sense and in its true meaning. That is why in the Economic Recovery Plan, specific provision was made for helping to promote the circulation of American publications and American ideas in Europe.

22 International Public Opinion Research, *A Report on Attitudes toward the United States and on Exposure to the Mass Media and to the United States Information Program in Chile*, a report submitted to the Office of Research and Evaluation, United States Information Agency, January, 1954.

covered radio, television, motion pictures, newspapers, magazines and books. It concluded:

> The data certainly do not prove but they suggest the reasonable hunch that the US and Russia, 'seen' as the principal contenders in the world scene today are also somewhat more suspect with regard to their propaganda output.[23]

There was certainly cause for the US Government to worry about the political stability of Latin America after the war. The chronic foreign exchange shortages of many Latin American countries had made it impossible to satisfy the rising demands of their populations. Populist leaders like Perón in Argentina, Vargas in Brazil, and Rojas Pinilla in Colombia were losing their dynamism and political support. In their desperation they often resorted to harsh censorship and control of the media. Although newspapers suffered the most, radio journalists, magazines, popular entertainers, and musicians also felt the regimes' heavy hand. When the populist regimes fell – Vargas in 1954, Perón in 1955, Rojas Pinilla in 1957 – their attempts to censor and, at the same time protect the development of domestic media industries through tariffs, subsidies, and state ownership collapsed. The years following their departure brought a period of sustained commercial expansion of the Latin American media, often with US investment, advertising, and news and entertainment content.

In the 1950s, the US television networks followed the same investment routes in Latin America as they had in their radio operations twenty and thirty years before. The national chapters describe the importance of these investments in the television industries in the different domestic markets. According to some analysts (Read, 1976, 78), these investments were not commercially successful from the point of view of the US companies:

> In sum, American broadcast executives were what stockbrokers would call 'bullish' about the prospects of investing in the international television market. Because they had the know-how, Americans were optimistic. But in the end there would only be potential deals, bad deals, and short-term training advisory contracts. With a few minor exceptions, nationalism would prompt foreign governments to deny outsiders control of the sensitive and powerful medium of television. By the end of the 1960s, America's involvement in television abroad would be restricted almost entirely to programme sales, and even there the industry would have reached a plateau.

Although Read considers the activities of the US networks in Latin America unprofitable from a commercial point of view, until 1970, when the US Federal Communications Commission placed restrictions on network syndication and separated the networks from most international sales, the international program-

---

23 United States Information Service, American Embassy, Rio de Janeiro, *Media Habits in Selected Brazilian Cities: Media, Overlap and Attitudes toward Propaganda*, Brazilian Public Opinion Surveys, Series 4, Report 8, March 1, 1957, 14.

ming sales of the US TV networks were profitable. Perhaps more important, however, the impact of the networks' investments on the the domestic Latin American broadcasting industries, was significant.

Both NBC and CBS had investments in the major Latin American television markets. ABC, however, a relative newcomer, regarded the potential of the international market on an even greater scale. Starting about 1960, ABC invested abroad, and established foreign affiliations with a network they called Worldvision. By 1964 ABC had 48 affiliated stations in 21 countries, including a Central American sub-regional network of television stations. In addition to the problems facing the other networks in their international expansion like national sensitivities to foreign investments in broadcasting, ABC found it was unable to attract advertisers to its concept of a worldwide investment strategy through its affiliates. ABC did continue as a sales representative and programme buying agent for some Latin American stations (Read 1976, 81).

The foreign investments of Time-Life television were similar to those of ABC. The company had entered in domestic television ownership in the United States relatively late and was anxious to take the lead in going international. Some of this expansion was financed by the foreign earnings of its magazines, which could be invested abroad advantageously. In partnership with Goar Mestre, director of Cuban television before the revolution, and CBS, Time-Life backed Latin American TV-production companies set up to get around domestic limitations on foreign investment – Proartel in Argentina, Proventel in Caracas. Later, Time-Life invested directly in TV Globo in Brazil. Read observes, in what to many could appear a revisionist theory that,

> ... looking back to the period of attempted and fruitless American investments in foreign television stations ... the few deals that were made, principally in Latin America, turned out to be costly mistakes for the US investors who discovered belatedly that their local partners desired American capital and know-how, nothing else. Once those ingredients had been transferred, the Americans were virtually powerless to reap any benefits from less than scrupulous indigenous partners and nationalist governments (90).

Even US imported programming soon lost its allure. American films were popular among more educated audiences. When audiences grew to encompass larger sectors of the middle class, and domestic industries learned how to produce their own, more popular, brands of musicals, soap operas and documentaries, US exports became limited to the more technically sophisticated and costly action and adventure series.

Although, as Read observes, foreign investment in Latin American television, for its immediate authors was ultimately unsuccessful and probably unprofitable in the long run, its impact on the Latin American broadcasting industries was significant. It succeeded in conveying an image and model of commercial broadcasting as the norm, and ultimate standard against which all other models were judged. Yet, this influence did not fall in a vacuum. The authoritarian and other regimes in the region mediated the impact of foreign programming and capital. Latin

American states supported politically docile, commercial media that did not present a challenge to the regimes in power. The eight national chapters analyse these processes of national mediation. Their findings show how the actions of the foreign state and industry are mediated through domestic actors. These processes are explored in the chapters that follow.

2 National policies of broadcasting

The national policies of broadcasting in each Latin American country were the result of the conflicts and accommodations among the different actors that accompanied the growth of local broadcasting industries. The main domestic policy actors were the state, the industry, and, although largely ignored in the long run, broader social movements. In addition, outside forces in the form of foreign capital, media, and governments, like those described in chapter 1, often swayed the course of domestic media development.

As the country case studies that follow show, the political elites of the region had little concept of a different role for their broadcasting media other than that provided by the US commercial broadcasting industry. Domestic industries in the region gravitated towards the model that was easiest, closest, and most beneficial to them, and this was commercial broadcasting. In societies already with significant amounts of foreign investment from US companies, broadcasting became a part of free enterprise, a market economy, and a natural vehicle for advertising and profit.

Because of the weaknesses of the Latin American state and the often undemocratic nature of national governments, political elites usually were more concerned with political censorship of the media than with establishing a social or public role for broadcasting or with giving broader social movements a say in the media's organisation. Institutions like the Church and universities, with some exceptions, left radio and television technologies to develop in the commercial orbit, failing to provide another vision of how the new broadcasting technologies might be organised to fit social demands like education, community building, or cultural expression. The prime concerns of the elites were economic growth and political stability, and a docile commercial broadcasting system satisfied both.

Although initial broadcasting policies in the region were largely liberal, in some countries a nationalist perspective emerged. This included policies advocating state control over domestic radio and television, measures to insure domestic content, and state interventions to insure the social application and the access of different sectors of the population to broadcasting services. Historically, these attempts at nationalist broadcasting policies on the part of Latin American states were successful when motivated by authoritarian and national security concerns, but largely unsuccessful when motivated by distributive concerns or considerations of 'national culture.'

Today, few Latin American states would advocate policies of protectionism or cultural nationalism for their national broadcasting industries. This is partly because the domestic media are competing strongly in international export markets, and partly the result of the combination of liberal economics and democratisation. Furthermore, some monopolistic national broadcasting industries have now grown stronger than the state. It is possible, however, that with the entrance of foreign capital, domestic monopolies will begin to feel competition, starting yet another cycle of demands for state protection. On the other hand, the increased internationalisation of the Latin American broadcasting industries themselves decreases the likelihood of a call for protectionist barriers.

By way of introduction to the chapters that follow, this chapter summarises some of the broader characteristics of domestic broadcasting policies in Latin America.

Early nationalist policies and prevailing commercialism

Nationalist policies in broadcasting were present early on in many Latin American countries. These policies, however, disappeared in the face of interests supporting a predominant image of commercial broadcasting. In Mexico, the first two decades of broadcasting's development occurred at a time of considerable state interest in the promotion of national culture and education, the result of the social reforms and nationalist aims of the Mexican Revolution, including the cultural and economic integration of Mexico's vast Indian populations in the national market and new society. The Mexican state under Education Secretary José Vasconcellos encouraged the growth of Mexican literature, art, and other forms of expression, and used culture to promote a sense of national unity and identity. The state paid for the great Mexican muralists – Rivera, Siqueiros, Orozco – to paint the walls of government buildings and owned the country's principal film studios, the majority of the movie theatres, and the bank financing most film production.

Despite the revolutionary government's interest in the promotion of national education and culture, however, the Mexican State paid little attention to the newer broadcasting technologies, perhaps because they did not fit with their 'Enlightenment' concept of culture. Two years after experimental broadcasts of radio in 1921, the government authorised the first commercial broadcasting licenses, mostly to newspaper publishers, who began to operate them as commercial enterprises.

There was, however, some effort to establish a public or state-owned broadcasting sector. In 1924 the Mexican government set up a radio station in the Ministry of Education. Ten years later, President Lázaro Cárdenas (1934–1940) donated a radio receiver to every agricultural and workers community to enable them to listen to the courses, book reviews, and concerts transmitted by the state radio station. These state-owned radio stations later were sold to private companies.

Peru, like Mexico a country with a large Indian population, underwent a period of social ferment and national cultural redefinition and reform in the 1920s and 1930s. The American Popular Revolutionary Alliance, APRA, a political party, was born, based on the rejection of foreign political, cultural, and social models. José

Carlos Mariátegui founded the Peruvian Socialist Party with a programme for Peruvian culture that recognised the central role of indigenous cultural forms in national development and identity. Peruvian radio stations, however, did not take part in the nationalist movements for cultural reform because no Peruvian radio station was allowed on the air until 1935, ten years after President Leguia established a government station, the Peruvian Broadcasting Company, that soon after was acquired by the Marconi Company and operated commercially.

In Uruguay, early state interest in radio was part of national educational and cultural policies. Uruguay was a prosperous, politically stable country in the 1930s, and the state could afford to finance media and the arts as well as other public services for its small, urban middle-class population. In 1929 the Uruguayan State set up a non-commercial public broadcasting service, SODRE (Servicio Oficial de Difusión Radio Eléctrico) with one state-financed shortwave and two medium wave frequencies. In addition to broadcasting, SODRE's activities included the National Symphony Orchestra, the Uruguayan National Ballet, and a film club operating in its own theatre. The state, however, did not limit the growth of private commercial media. Economic prosperity and the high educational level of the population made it possible for many small commercial radio stations to thrive, building audiences attractive to advertisers and financing their operations with commercials. By the 1950s this commercial broadcasting sector was sufficiently powerful to block the further expansion of state-owned media.

Commercial broadcasting was prevalent from the beginning of the century in Argentina, Colombia, and Chile. The urban consolidation of Buenos Aires facilitated the precocious expansion of private broadcasting, allowing stations to reach the dense urban markets with little effort. In 1923 the Ministry of the Navy issued five radio licenses to private radio stations in the capital serving an audience of about 60,000 radio sets. The government passed the administration of the radio licenses to the Ministry of the Post and Telegraph in 1928 and enacted the first law regulating private, public, and amateur radio stations. Ten years later forty-two radio stations spanned the country, many of them affiliated with one of two commercial radio networks.

Colombian radio made up for its relatively late birth in 1929 by growing rapidly after 1931 when a president from the Liberal Party changed the tax system to make commercial operations of radio stations profitable. Using a formula particular to Colombia, and later applied to television, radio became a public-private hybrid. The Colombian government franchised time slots on state-owned radio stations to private companies who exploited them commercially by selling advertising time. Commercial and amateur radio stations lent their services to the Colombian government in a 1932 war with Peru, helping consolidate a system of commercially – rather than state-operated radio.

During the 1930s, a period of national industrialisation, urbanisation, and foreign investment throughout the hemisphere, radio stations met the advertising needs of domestic and foreign industries. In 1935 Colombian manufacturers of tobacco products, textiles, beer, foodstuffs, and pharmaceutical companies grouped together to set up a large regional radio station on which they could advertise their products. The seventeen private commercial radio stations registered in Colombia in 1934 jumped to 42 stations by 1939, and, two years later, to 70.

During a period of national industrialisation in the early 1930s a market for goods that could be advertised on commercial radio likewise began to form in Chile. Despite state interests in education and the arts – the Chilean State had undertaken the expansion of the national education system, arts, and culture like the national symphony and opera companies – the government did not subsidise the nascent mass media. Left on their own without government subsidies or state-ownership, Chilean media developed an early commercial character, catering to the demands and tastes of audience of the newly forming urban markets.

Government censorship, however, quickly was added to the Latin American version of private commercial broadcasting. In some countries the state imposed controls on the political content of the media through censorship and limits on licenses. This was the case of Brazil in the 1930s under Vargas, Argentina during the 'decade infame,' and the first years of radio in Peru.

Statist efforts at broadcasting policies

In the late 1950s and early 1960s Latin American countries were buffeted by severe economic problems and mounting social pressures. Within the general thinking on development, some of the earlier ideas about the role of cultural expression and communication in national development came back in vogue. This time, rather than the idea of integrating a culturally heterogeneous nation, emphasis of this school of development communication was on the use of the newer audiovisual technologies to provide education, information, and modern values to the 'traditional' masses.[1] International development programmes like the Alliance for Progress and the Organisation of American States made funds available for communication equipment and programmes to use the mass media in health, education, rural development, and family planning. Recipients of aid received educational radio and television systems, communication satellites, and vast agricultural extension programmes.

The readiness of the United States and other countries to grant Latin American governments large amounts of direct economic aid benefited the expansion of the development communication systems. In 1966, using foreign funds, Colombian President Carlos Lleras set up an educational television programme in coordination with the Ministry of Education as a complement to regular classroom programmes. He also established a programme of grassroots integration and rural development using television to reach lower-income adults. In 1968 the Mexican government began an open-circuit educational television system for secondary school called Telesecundaria. These state-directed development policies were by and large complementary to commercial broadcasting and non-conflictive. Many of the redistributive attempts that grew out of them, however, were highly controversial. These attempts, largely to establish some sort of state-broadcasting sector, raised bitter controversy among the private sector and rival political factions and ended in failure.

---

1   See for example: Lerner (1958), Pye (1963), Schramm (1964), Schramm and Lerner (1964). For a later example of this school, McAnany (1980).

The triumph of commercialism

With the failure of many development efforts, the disappearance of most foreign funding for development, and the endorsement of free market economics by many of the military dictatorships, a liberal perspective returned to Latin America in force in the 1970s. It has continued up to the present with the advent of the 'neo-liberal' economic policies advocating the reduction of state regulation and owner-ship of the media and the removal of restrictions on the commercial operations of most domestic as well as foreign media, often in association with regional 'free-trade agreements.'

The liberal image for media has been reinforced by the return of democratical-ly elected governments. Republican liberalism, based on the image of the pluralist nature of society in which individuals and groups compete freely to capture the state, supports private commercial media as a necessary and defining component of democracy. By the time of the second liberal revival, the Latin American commer-cial broadcasting media were in a position to consolidate large domestic monopo-lies, many with considerable international holdings and sizable export activities.

Marxist policies

Marxist-inspired broadcasting policies in Latin America in which state control of the media replaces any private or commercial forms are largely absent from the cases analysed in this book. Marxist-inspired policies were applied fully only in Cuba after the 1959 Revolution. The Cuban private commercial media were placed under state control and put at the service of the revolution and its goals of culture, education, and defence of revolutionary programmes. These policies were applied partially under Salvador Allende in Chile, although mainly in the field of publish-ing, and in Nicaragua under the Sandinistas, mainly in regard to television. Policies in these countries, however, never achieved the strength they did in Cuba.

Marxist-inspired policies in some cases came close to those advocated by real-ists or nationalists.[2] While nationalist policies advocated state ownership of media to protect against other states and insure national development, Marxist-inspired policies advocated state ownership to protect against the evils of capitalism and class interests.

The national chapters

The national chapters look at the broadcasting policies of eight Latin American countries. They examine the domestic forces and interests that established and developed radio and television industries and the role of the state in this process. Each country chapter analyses the accommodations and conflicts among social groups, economic interests, political parties, and the state, and the policy debates that have occurred throughout most of the twentieth century over the ownership, purpose and content of radio and television broadcasting.

---

2   Gilpin (1987, p.43) observes that Marxism at times becomes nearly indistinguishable from political realism. 'However', he states, 'the assumptions of the two theories regarding the basis of human motivation, the theory of the state, and the nature of the international system are fundamentally different. Marxists regard human nature

The evolution of national broadcasting policies in the eight countries demonstrates a number of similarities. At different periods in each country the state needed more access to and control over the media in order to accomplish political objectives, and was able to exert control over commercial media ownership and content. At others times, governments initiated state-directed national policies within broader political and economic reforms, ostensibly focusing on broadcasting's foreign 'dependency' and lack of role in social and economic development, but ultimately more concerned with domestic political control. These economic and social redistributive policies largely disappeared since the late 1970s, first under authoritarian dictatorships and, later, under the new liberal intellectual climate that limited the role of the public sector, tightened fiscal and monetary politics, and expanded free-market economics.

The chapters show domestic communication policies in Latin America were not primarily the result of 'nationalist' sentiments, concerned with the protection of national interests or culture. Nor were policies motivated exclusively by liberal economic philosophies of free markets or the democratic republicanism of a free press. Domestic broadcasting policies and the ways in which radio and television industries evolved in the countries were to a large degree the result of the characteristics of domestic political power and its interaction with the radio and television industries.

When domestic political forces were able to reach an accommodation with national broadcasting industries, strong media monopolies developed; this is the case of Mexico, Brazil and Venezuela. Here, the broadcasting media have acquired their own political power and autonomy from the state, and acquired an ability to operate outside any national policy guideline. When accommodations between the state and the industry were not forthcoming, the broadcasting industry remained politically weaker and generally more fragmented, historically the case of Colombia, Argentina, and Peru. In all three of these countries this fragmentation is beginning to dissipate and monopolies are forming with stronger political roles for the media. Likewise, Chile and Uruguay failed to forge a bond between a strong state and a domestic broadcasting power under either democratic or authoritarian regimes. Today their national broadcasting institutions are in transition, with renegotiations underway among the principal actors.

As the case studies show, the challenge facing Latin American societies today in the organisation of their domestic communication systems is not to 'free' these of foreign influence, capital, or technology. The challenge is to provide a different relationship or accommodation regarding the media and their control among the different domestic actors. This accommodation would mean a new conception of the rights and obligations of the state – through its institutions of political representation – and of the increasingly autonomous, powerful, and transnational domestic media industries.

These wider considerations of rights and obligations, political representation and accountability, have been largely absent from broadcasting policies throughout the region. The demands of social movements and grassroots organisations for greater political participation and cultural representation have by and large proved short-lived. The Mexican government, temporarily shaken by popular protests and demands for wider political participation, felt the need to reaccommodate its relationship with the private media. The state-driven reforms, however, ultimately led to the development of government media channels rather than increased 'democratisation' of the media. Similar pressures for increased popular representation contributed to the Chilean government's initial decision to set up a national television network, yet ultimately resulted in increased government control. Peru's top-down media reform lead to an enormous government media bureaucracy with little real popular input.

Possibilities for achieving goals of democratisation of the media are different in each country. Brazil, Mexico, and Venezuela, with the strongest private monopolies, probably face the toughest challenge. As the previously fragmented media race to form larger multi-media conglomerates in Colombia and Argentina, it is unclear which will prevail: the autonomy of the media or the strength of fragile democratic organs of representation. The situation in Uruguay and Chile is more open-ended. The commitment to popular representation and political participation in the media in these newly consolidating democracies, however, faces new obstacles of increased control of the media by the larger Latin American media monopolies. Each country presents a different array of circumstances, the result of the historical development of the media in that society.

3 *Mexico*

The Mexican state early on formed a close relationship with private commercial broadcasters. Mexican broadcasters freely developed the commercial operations of radio and television and did not challenge the state politically. This relationship made authoritarian measures to control domestic (or foreign) broadcasting in Mexico largely unnecessary. From the initial days of radio to the present monopoly of Televisa, the accommodations between the Mexican state and the domestic broadcasting industry evolved within a framework of mutual benefit. This basic 'partnership' between the state and broadcasters was and continues to be the dominant characteristic of Mexican broadcasting. It was made possible by the control of the Mexican state by one party, the Partido Revolucionario Institucional (PRI) during the entire period of commercial broadcasting's growth.

US investments were present in Mexico from the initial days of radio and continued through the introduction and spread of television, especially in export activities and, later, in the direct involvement of Mexican broadcasters in the US Hispanic media market. One must look to the domestic relationship between the radio and television industries and the Mexican government, however, rather than to foreign relations, to understand the evolution of Mexican broadcasting.

Sporadic conflicts and a need to re-accommodate the relationship between the Mexican state and the broadcasting industry arose in response to changing social and political demands of the Mexican people. In the long run, these popular demands were largely ignored or excluded from broadcasting policies, partly as a result of the increasing dependence of the ruling party on the private commercial broadcasting industry for public relations and political advertising.

Televisa, the Mexican media monopoly, is the product of the long, successful relationship between the Mexican media and the country's political leaders. Today, Televisa covers 96 per cent of the national territory, produces over 35,000 hours of television yearly, exports programmes to 50 countries, and transmits via satellite twenty-four hours daily to the United States. ECO, its news service with over 100 correspondents throughout the world, transmits via satellite 24 hours a day to 47 countries on three continents.

The introduction of radio

Mexican broadcasting was not born commercial but as a mixture of private and public enterprises. Following the turmoil of the Mexican Revolution, the initial broadcasting policies of the Mexican state were similar to policies applied in other sectors of the economy, a mixture of state and private enterprise. The state supported and subsidised the development of a private broadcasting sector while at the same time building some state-owned media.

The first two decades of radio's development were a time of considerable government interest in the promotion of national culture and education, the result of social reforms and nationalist aims of the Mexican Revolution, including the cultural and economic integration of Mexico's vast Indian populations. The Mexican state used cultural forms to promote a sense of national unity and identity, financing the murals on the walls of government buildings and owning the country's principal film studios, most movie theatres, and the bank financing most films. In 1924 the Mexican government set up a radio station in the Ministry of Education. Later, the ruling party established two radio stations of its own. Yet, despite three state-owned stations radio – one from the Ministry of Education and two from the ruling Partido Nacional Revolucionario (which later became the PRI) – Mexican public or government broadcasting did not survive for long.

The government awarded the first commercial broadcasting licenses in 1923, and many were given to Mexican newspaper publishers. In 1932 ten commercial radio stations were operating in Mexico City and twenty stations in cities in the interior of the country. Many stations were clustered along the northern border, targeting an audience already accustomed to receiving radio broadcasts from the United States. The private radio stations' growing earnings from advertising allowed them to finance live comedy, dramas, folk music, sports events, and the enormously popular radio novelas, the Latin America brand of soap operas.

Foreign capital and technology entered Mexican broadcasting during its early development. Emilio Azcárraga, a distributor of the Radio Corporation of America, RCA, in Mexico City, inaugurated radio station XEW in 1930 as an affiliate of the National Broadcasting Company, NBC. In 1938, Azcárraga began radio station XEQ, affiliated with the Columbia Broadcasting System, CBS, and soon formed a chain of seventeen stations throughout the country.

Mexico's early, although unequal, mix between state and private ownership in the economy, including broadcasting, however, did not last. The year 1940 was a watershed year in Mexican politics. General Avila Camacho, a political moderate, became president, dashing the hopes of those sectors of the ruling party who wanted to continue to expand the social reforms begun after the revolution and increase the role of the Mexican state in the national economy. A new cast of professional politicians replaced the old revolutionary generals. President Miguel Alemán (1946-1952) was the first civilian present elected after the Revolution. His policies profoundly changed the relationship between the Mexican state and the private sector by decreasing direct state ownership and increasing support to private enterprise. After 1941 the Mexican state divested itself of its radio stations, leaving radio to develop commercially. The government and the ruling party closed down their radio stations or sold them to private investors. At the same time, the state continued to subsidise private broadcasters with import exemptions, subsidised electricity tariffs, and scholarships to train broadcasting personnel.

The relationship between the Mexican state and private broadcasters was friendly. Private broadcasters worked closely with the government in communications policy and often formed part of official delegations to intergovernmental telecommunications conferences. After 1940, for example, private broadcasters regularly were part of official Mexican delegations to the conventions of the International Telecommunications Union, giving the private sector a voice in the international agreements signed by the Mexican government.

Likewise, Mexican commercial broadcasters were active in international organisations for the defence and promotion of private commercial broadcasting. In 1946 they were founding members of the Asociacion Interamericana de Radio Difusion (AIR), and of Televisión Asociada, an organisation of Latin American radio broadcasters set up to lobby governments throughout the region for the introduction of commercial television.

By the time television reached Mexico in the mid-1950s, commercial radio broadcasting had eclipsed any public or state-owned activity. Private commercial radio had enjoyed almost 25 years of sustained administrative and technical experience and economic growth, and the Mexican state had abandoned almost all its own direct activities in the field of broadcasting.

The introduction of television

In 1947 President Miguel Alemán gave the National Institute of Fine Arts the task of studying the two principal television models in the world – the BBC and the US private television networks. It came as no surprise when the report came out firmly in favour of a framework for privately owned Mexican television. On the basis of the report's recommendations, Aleman distributed the first three licenses to operate commercial television channels. A license for Channel 4 was given to Romulo O'Farril, the owner of the newspaper *Novedades* in Mexico City. It appeared on the air in September 1950 with a transmission of President Alemán's State of the Union Address. Channel 2 was awarded to radio owner Emilio Azcárraga. Engineer and inventor Gonzalez Camarena received a license to operate Channel 5.

Much of the transmission and studio equipment and many of the feature films and TV series shown on the three channels were imported from the United States. (Both Azcárraga and Camarena had long-standing commercial relations with the US radio and television networks.) In 1955, after an initial period of competition, the three channels joined together to form Telesistema Mexicano.[1] By 1959 Telesistema Mexicano operated 20 channels throughout the country. Although virtually a monopoly, the channels had developed their own audiences and programming styles, thereby preserving the appearance of a competitive broadcasting market. Channel 2 specialised in Mexican-produced variety and game shows, dramas, and international news. Channel 4, aimed at lower-income audiences, showed soap operas, dubbed films, sports, and local news. Channel 5 targeted children with cartoons and adventure series, most of which it imported from the United States.

---

1 The new company operated Channels 2, 4 and 5, although the licenses remained in the names of their original owners. In this way, Telesistema complied with Article 28 of the Mexican Constitution prohibiting monopolies.

Telesistema adopted the latest technologies of television production and transmission, again mostly imported from the United States. It acquired the new video technologies from Ampex, a US company, and Channel 2 transmitted its first programmes recorded on video in 1959. In addition to reducing costs and improving the quality of productions, the new video technologies enabled Telesistema Mexicano to begin to export television programmes throughout Latin America and to the United States. Mexican broadcasters developed an international base for their operations in association with US television channels serving Hispanic markets. Telesistema set up a production company, Teleprogramas de Mexico, to export programmes, and in 1966 formed Teleprogramas Acapulco to produce soap operas for Mexican and export markets. One-quarter of the production company was owned by the American Broadcasting Company, ABC. The director of Teleprogramas was Miguel Alemán Velasco, the son of President Miguel Alemán, who was part owner of Telesistema.

Although the Mexican state had withdrawn from the direct ownership of radio and television stations, it continued to subsidise the expansion of the private broadcasting sector. One the main concerns of the private television channels in Mexico City was the transmission of signals to other regions of the country. The Mexican government began construction of a national microwave system in 1955. By 1958 three routes were in operation. In order to provide national coverage for the 1968 Olympic Games held in Mexico City, the government constructed a high-capacity microwave network between Mexico City and the United States border and a satellite ground station to send to ATS-6, the experimental NASA satellite. Based in part on its use of the government-constructed infrastructure, Telesistema grew to become the largest network in the country, affiliating thirty-seven stations by the end of the 1960s.

Although by far the largest, Telesistema was not the only Mexican television network. In 1968 a license to operate Channel 12 in Monterrey was awarded to Manuel Barbachano Ponce, a Mexican film producer. His company, Telecadena Mexicana, operated eight stations in the north, centre, and southeast of the country. That same year, the industrial group ALFA of Monterrey was awarded a license to operate Channel 8 in Mexico City under the name Televisión Independiente de México. The two Monterrey companies operated as a network in the capital city and north of the country. In Mexico City, Francisco Aguirre, the owner of a radio chain, received a license, to operate Channel 13.

The legal framework of broadcasting

The legal framework of Mexican television, dating from an earlier period when state and private media ownership were more balanced, hardly kept pace with commercial broadcasting's rapid growth. In 1940 the Law of Communication (Vias Generales) gave the government exclusive regulatory jurisdiction over broadcasting and barred foreigners from owning Mexican broadcasting licenses. The Ministry of Communication and Public Works was authorised to grant concessions and permits and establish technical regulations for the general operations of radio stations. When necessary, the ministry could revoke broadcasting licenses and expropriate installations, but it had no power to dictate programming content.

In 1960 the Federal Broadcasting Law changed the definition of Mexican radio and television from 'public services' to 'services of public interest'. The law set general guidelines for television content like the promotion of national values and the harmonic development of children. It prohibited the transmission of news or propaganda threatening public order or national security. Reversing the 1940 Law, the 1960 Law gave private license holders total freedom to set advertising rates and times, although it set some guidelines for advertising like limitations on the advertising of alcoholic beverages.[2]

At the same time the Mexican Government relaxed restriction on advertising, it passed a new tax bill with a 5 per cent tax on the gross earnings of radio and television stations. It was the first time the earnings of broadcasters had been taxed, and was probably agreed upon by the private broadcasters in exchange for the easing of the regulations on advertising. Following negotiations between the Secretary of the Treasury and the Mexican National Association of Broadcasters, the new tax later was lowered to 1.25 per cent.

Mexican state broadcasting

Throughout the consolidation of Mexican commercial broadcasting, the Mexican state depended almost exclusively on the private sector to provide information and communication services between the government and the Mexican people. This 'dependency' did not constitute a problem because of the close relationship between the state and the private broadcasters and the absence of other political parties competing for media coverage. State radio stations were sold or disbanded by the early 1940s. One small public television channel, Channel 11, founded in 1959 in the Politechnical Institute, barely covered the northeastern sector of Mexico City.

With the exception of educational television,[3] Mexico's broadcasting was solidly commercial. Radio and television were no longer defined as public services, and the state had little say in the way they were run. The broadcasting law of 1960, the main instrument of broadcasting policy, was largely the creation of private industry. Given the close ties between the state, the ruling party, and the owners of commercial broadcasting, no crack appeared in this arrangement until the late 1960s.

A debate over national communication policies

A debate over national communication policies and a movement to set up a state-owned broadcasting sector in Mexico began in the late 1960s in the context of a severe national economic crisis and a series of state-imposed fiscal austerity measures. Growing popular discontent was partially responsible for the state's need for national communication policies and for the formation of its own information and public opinion resources. The debates over domestic media policies continued through the period of Mexican oil wealth in the late 1970s. Throughout this

---

2 The author of much of the 1960 Federal Broadcasting Law was Jose Luis Fernandez, owner of the radio station XELA. With Justino Jimenez Arechiga of Uruguay, Fernandez wrote a project to standardise Latin American legislation on broadcasting – *12 Bases de la AIR para Uniformar la Primera Legislación Interamericana de Radiodifusión.* Much of the 1960 Mexican Broadcasting law was based on the 12 points proposed in the AIR document.

3 In 1965 the Secretary of Public Education began a pilot literacy project using television, and in 1968 a small government educational television system, Telesecundaria, went on the air.

period, although the national economy grew at an annual rate of about 5 per cent, the standard of living of most Mexicans continued to fall.

As a result of Mexico's economic difficulties, for the first time since the early days after the Mexican Revolution, PRI, the ruling party faced a crisis of legitimacy. New political movements questioned PRI's traditional control of elections and the machinery of government. Powerful industrial groups openly resisted the government's policy of nationalisation and threatened the country's economic stability with massive withdrawals of private capital. Social groups, long deprived of access and participation in the political and economic life of the country, menaced the stability of the system with strikes, protests, and armed guerrilla struggles. The student movement was brutally put down in 1968. Other grassroots protests suffered repression from the state and from extreme right-wing organisations.

When President Luis Echeverría Alvarez (1970-1976) took office in December 1970, Mexico was in the throes of severe political conflicts, labour protests, and simmering rural unrest, for the most part the result of the slowly deteriorating wages of the Mexican workers and their lack of real channels of political participation. Echeverría began a programme of political reform, intended mainly to contain the dissident movements and bring them into the mainstream of Mexican politics. The reforms continued through 1982 during the administration of President José Lopez Portillo (1976-1982).

The reforms contained political as well as cultural measures. Changes in the electoral system strengthened independent political parties and labour movements. Other political parties, including the Mexican Communist party, were legalised and given the political rights guaranteed them under the Mexican Constitution. Government measures supported a more critical and independent domestic film industry and invited dissident intellectuals and artists to work within the government.

The cultural and broadcasting reforms were to a large degree the result of the political crisis. In part, the government used the private media as a scapegoat to blame for their failures and in part they felt they no longer could trust the private media to be their loyal mouthpiece. The ruling party called for a new use of the mass media, freeing the state from its thirty-year self-imposed dependence on the private media and returning to the earlier balance between private and state-owned media. By 1986, as a result of new policies, state television could reach audiences similar to those of the private stations. Within the following five years, however, with the calming of the political crisis and the re-establishment of the good relationship between the ruling party and commercial broadcasters, these measures would be reversed.

Government controls on the private media

The government policy measures began with a new tax on broadcasters and a government advertising campaign criticising negative aspects of commercial broadcasting like violence and consumerism and praising the positive aspects of a public broadcasting system like educational and cultural aims. The campaign blamed advertising and the programming shown on the commercial media for many of the serious economic and cultural problems facing the country, including excess spending and cultural alienation.

In 1974, speaking at the opening of a world communications meeting in Acapulco, President Echeverría had strong words for the mercenary management of private radio and television: 'We will have to consider the media a threat as long as they support an absurd and unjust economic system that survives by inventing needs, squandering essential resources, and ignoring the real necessities of three-quarters of the population' (Echevarría 1974).

The government set up a National Consumers Institute to analyse advertising and conduct consumer education programmes. The campaign against the use of televised violence reached a high point in 1974 when President Echeverría's state of the union address accused televised violence of contributing to the armed guerrilla movements operating in the country. The 1969 National Tax Law levied a 25 per cent tax on the payments made by advertisers, agencies, and programme producers to private broadcasters for air time, studio use, and equipment rentals. Article 16 of the law gave private broadcasters the option of paying the tax or of becoming public companies and putting 49 per cent of their stock up for sale, either directly or through government-owned credit institutions. Neither of the options suited private broadcasters, and the government and industry negotiated a third option. In July 1969, by presidential decree, in exchange for the 25 per cent tax on earnings, the government accepted 12.5 per cent of the transmission time of the commercial channels for the transmission of government programmes. The government used this time to transmit official communiques and public services, including educational television. The same year a presidential decree set aside thirty-seven television channels throughout the country for official use. Three years later Echeverría inaugurated the Mexican Cultural Television System.

The decree setting up the cultural television system argued that most television channels served urban areas. Therefore, the state had the obligation to bring television to the rural areas to make this powerful instrument of communication an effective vehicle of national integration and culture. The Mexican state, however, had no facilities with which to produce programming for their new cultural TV channels. The decree setting up the system stipulated that the content would consist of programming produced by state channels and those programmes of Mexican commercial channels deemed appropriate for cultural broadcasts. The government agreed to transmit the original advertisements along with the programmes it used from the private channels.[4]

In 1972 the Mexican state acquired the Corporación Mexicana de Radio y Televisión, Channel 13, a commercial television station operating in Mexico City that was near bankruptcy. Channel 13's programming schedule was changed from movie reruns and imported series to government information programmes. After 1978, soap operas, variety shows, musicals, and sports were added to Channel 13's regular broadcasts. The Mexican government built new studios for Channel 13 and recruited progressive intellectuals to provide quality programming, many of whom, disturbed by government censorship, eventually left. Beginning in 1982 Channel 13 accepted some advertising.

---

4 By 1972 the cultural television system had 110 affiliates. It reached communities of between 10,000 and 20,000 inhabitants and had an audience of about a million and a half people.

The growth of monopoly and re-accommodation between the state and the private sector

During the first years of the Mexican government's (re)entrance into broadcasting, the private sector openly and aggressively opposed the state-owned media and countered the government's moves against private broadcasters with their own publicity campaigns and other measures. In 1973, the two largest Mexican private broadcasters, faced with what they considered the dangerous, left-wing tendencies of the Echeverría administration's expansion into broadcasting, joined forces. Telesistema Mexicano, owned by Azcárraga, Alemán and O'Farril, the original television licensees in Mexico City, joined with Television Independiente de Mexico, owned by the Monterrey group from the industrialised north. The new firm, called Televisa, Television Via Satellite, constituted a virtual national monopoly of Mexican private broadcasting.

Each of the channels of the new company was clearly differentiated, again giving the Mexican public the sensation of choice, even though all channels were owned by the same company. Channel 2 was the 'quality' channel, producing and transmitting soap operas and variety shows domestically and throughout Latin America and the United States. Channel 4, traditionally the channel for the lower-income audiences of Televisa, based its programming on reruns of Mexican and Latin American movies, series, variety shows, and some national sports and news. From 1977 on, Channel 4 (in payment of the 12.5 per cent time obligation) broadcast Telesecundaria, the state educational television programme. Channel 5 built its programming around imported cartoons and adventure series for children. In the evening it presented imported family programming and action and police adventure series. Channel 8, the flagship station of the Monterrey group, abandoned its 'competitive' programming and turned to movie reruns and imported series. In 1983, it became Televisa's cultural station.

After the merger Televisa expanded in the communications field both domestically and internationally. In 1976 Televisa acquired 20 per cent of the Spanish International Communication Corporation of the United States and set up Univision. Linked via satellite and microwave, Univision's channels in New York, Los Angeles, and San Antonio broadcast live Televisa programming and popular soap operas to Hispanic audiences in the United States.[5]

The newly consolidated private sector did not remain silent in face of government criticism of commercial broadcasting. Rather than promote consumerism, representatives of the private television industry claimed that one of their legally assigned functions was to contribute to the economic diversification and expansion of the economy through advertising (Vargas 1971). The Mexican National Association of Broadcasters argued that it was impossible to nationalise the private television stations because they already operated under a government license (Flores 1971). To counter presidential criticism of their activities, Mexican broadcasters aired a series of public relations spots entitled *Radio and Television are reliable, timely communication*. One spot announced that radio and television were part of Mexico's social, industrial, and commercial progress. Stations broadcast

---

5 In 1980 Televisa began using Westar, a US satellite, to transmit throughout Mexico and to stations in the United States. In 1984 Televisa acquired two trans-ponders on the Galaxy I satellite to transmit to the Galavision cable network in many US cities.

commercial messages that sell Mexican products and create Mexican jobs. Another explained that radio and television collaborate with the administration and maintain public order by bringing the voice of the government to the country.

By 1976, the defensive campaigns of the Mexican broadcasters had quieted. It was clear that the state would not abandon the expansion of its communication resources, but these posed little threat to the earnings or operations of the private sector. It was also clear that the ruling party still needed the private broadcasters. President José Lopez Portillo (1976-1982), addressing the private broadcasters shortly before his election, expressed a new tone of reconciliation with the private media and a recognition for their growing political importance: 'I count on you for my campaign. I will be present in every house to which you carry my image. I count on you in the fields and in the countryside. But more than anything, after the elections, if elected, I count on you for my presidency' (Lopez Portillo 1975).

In 1976 Miguel Alemán Velasco, son of the Mexican President who awarded the first TV licenses and soon-to-be president of Televisa's growing multi-media empire, expressed a conciliatory position of the private sector regarding government broadcasting. He explained that Mexico had achieved a mixed formula that allowed the different channels to perform different functions. Televisa's Channel 2 provided national communications; Channel 4 provided urban communications; Channel 5 provided world communications, and Channel 8 provided national feedback. The government's Channel 11 provided education, and Channel 13 provided culture. Finally, the 12.5 per cent time the government reserved on the private channels fulfiled the government's need to communicate with public opinion (Alemán 1976, 195). An accommodation one again had been reached between the ruling party and the private broadcasters.

In balance, the Mexican government's development of its own broadcasting resources served the needs of the ruling party for communication media without seriously challenging the profits or growth of the private sector. In the long run the state media indirectly subsidised the expansion of television into rural areas, relieved the private sector of its public service obligations, and sufficiently threatening the owners of television license to precipitate their merger and end their costly competition. Although the creation of state-owned broadcasting media resolved the Mexican government's historical lack of resources to get its own story out, it largely ignored participation and access to the media by the Mexican people. The government's response to demands for greater popular participation and access to the media was far less successful than its re-accommodation with the private sector and satisfaction of its own need for media resources.

The right to information

Upon taking office in 1976, the administration of José Lopez Portillo initiated a new television policy. The Basic Plan of the Government for 1976-1982 promised to carry out a careful review of both print and electronic media in order to guarantee the right to information of all members of Mexican society. The government plan declared the freedoms and liberties of all Mexicans were threatened if power, wealth, culture, and information were not equally distributed. The government presented the right to information as a way to overcome the mercenary and monopolistic conceptions of the mass media, enrich the people's knowledge, and guarantee democratic participation in the media. Upon taking office, Portillo declared it was necessary to put into effect the right to information in which the modern mass media have the duty to earn their freedom of expression by expressing themselves with freedom, responsibility, respect, and opportunity.

The right to information formed part of a larger political reform conceived by Jesús Reyes Heroles, Portillo's Interior Minister. It began as a measure permitting access to the mass media by the different political parties. Article 6 of the Federal Law of Political Organisations and Electoral Processes gave political parties equal access to the mass media to disseminate their opinions and programmes as guaranteed under Article 41 of the Mexican Constitution. In December 1977 the right to information was incorporated in Article 6 of the political reform. The new right guaranteed the right of all citizens to be informed and ensured their active role in the processes of communication. Portillo announced he would present a law guaranteeing the right to information, developing and regulating the new Article 6 of the Constitution.[6]

In October 1978 Reyes Heroles informed private broadcasters that freedom of expression was insufficient for the individual. Freedom of expression, he explained, implies the absence of the state. The right to information, on the other hand, implies an obligation on the part of the state and society to develop the necessary actions to satisfy the requirements of all individuals (Reyes 1978). In December of that year, however, Portillo announced a delay in the regulation of the right to information, calling for public hearings on the right with a wide range of different organisations. The regulation of the right, the president explained, should seek a balance between freedom of expression as an individual guarantee, and the right to information as a social guarantee. The delay in the regulation of the right to information was a sign of appeasement to the private sector. A further sign was provided in 1979 when the government suspended the 1.25 per cent tax on the gross earnings of radio and television licensees. In 1979 Portillo reaffirmed that an essential part of his overall political reform was the government's responsibility to defend everyone's access to the media.[7] Yet, in the same breath he named a new interior minister, Enrique Olivares Santana, removing Reyes Heroles, the outspoken proponent of the right to information.

In September 1980 the majority leader of the Chamber of Deputies announced a series of public hearings on the right to information. Political parties, professional associations, journalists, labour unions, universities, researchers, and community organisations signed up to voice their opinions on the right to information and its future regulation. One hundred and forty proposals were submitted to the Chamber of Deputies. Public hearings in Guadalajara, Hermosillo, Merida, Monterrey and Mexico City were held on four main points (Caletti 1988).[8]

---

6 Camera de Diputados, Mexico, 'Proceso Legislativo de la Reforma Politica, Iniciativa y Proyeto de Decreto, Compilacion de Diario de los Debates, December 1977, 8.

7 III Informe de Gobierno, September 1979.

8 These points were:

   a. The government's failure to fulfil its obligations to inform the people and the need to modify the government's communication behaviour to better inform the people and the media;

Although only 22 of the 140 proposals presented at the hearing opposed the right to information, the government declared that given the potential of any regulation to limit freedom of expression, it was preferable to leave the right to information unregulated. The government conclusion confessed: 'We have not found the formula to regulate the right to information; we have not found a way to square a circle' (Farias 1981). What the government had not found was a way to democratise the media and keep media owners happy at the same time.

The office of the president, however, continued to pursue the right to information. Portillo named Luis Javier Solana to head the Office of Coordination of Social Communication of the Presidency and charged him with elaborating a National Plan of Social Communication and a law regulating the right to information. Solana's plan recommended gradual measures to promote diversity and competition in the private sector, limit monopolies, and facilitate the growth of new communication institutions to meet the needs of the people. The plan proposed a National Communication Council to encourage wider social participation in the media. It also recommended the government gradually place its own communication resources under public control.[9]

Solana's far reaching plan advised the government to eliminate political subsidies to newspapers, set up national telecommunications industries, and rationalise the use of the airwaves. It recommended the development of cable TV and UHF, the regulation of advertising, and subsidises for national productions. Solana's plan was never officially released, although partial versions appeared in the Mexican press, where they set off a debate between the private media and the proponents of Solana's plan. Between 23 September and 30 December 1981, leading Mexican newspapers and magazines published 481 articles, editorials, and interviews on the proposed plan. Labour and peasant unions, miners, and the opposition political parties urged the government to regulate the right to information and enact a national plan of social communication. Opponents of the plan called it fascist, totalitarian, and communist, accusing the government of wanting to gag newspapers and restrict freedom of expression.

Portillo withdrew support for the controversial plan even before its official release. In October 1981 the president explained that it was difficult for the state to pass judgments on the right to information. The right to inform and to be informed was a passive right; individuals, the president felt, had to establish their own rules and assume their own commitments on the basis of their shared values (Lopez Portillo 1981). Solana resigned in February 1982 and was replaced by Francisco Galinda Ochoa, a member of the PRI who had served twice as the party's press secretary. Galinda cancelled all activities of the Office of Social Communications and fired its 150 employees and 50 researchers.[10] Galinda moved

b. The monopolistic development of the Mexican communication industries and the need to limit monopolies, regulate content, improve coverage, and decrease the influence of the transnational entertainment and news industries in the Mexican media;

c. The need to reorganise the legal structure of the Mexican information and cultural sector and protect and regulate the activities of professionals in the field;

d. The need to incorporate different social organisations in the structure of the media as owners of new media or with greater access to existing media.

9 *Revista Proceso*, (Mexico) 28 September 1981, 256.

10 *Proceso*, 10 February 1982, 10.

the Office of Social Communication in the direction of more traditional public relations activities and clamped down on opposition magazines and newspapers writing on political corruption and the government's manipulation of the election campaign of the PRI candidates.

Outcome of the re-accommodation

The Mexican government's initial expansion of state-owned broadcasting was the result of a domestic political need. It was not a response to wider social demands for participation and access to the media or a belief in the 'democratisation' of the media. Government ownership did not result automatically in the more democratic management of the media. The government retreated on its initial promise of reforms when social and political groups demanded access to privately controlled media as well as to the new state-owned media along with their own radio and television licenses and broadcasting time. Opposition to increased popular participation in the media came from the private media. The strongest opposition, however, came from within the ruling party itself, from those unwilling to risk losing control over the media and increasing real democratic participation. It was easier for the ruling party to reach an agreement with a monopolistic private broadcaster than to deal with a freer and more diversified domestic media environment. After the attempts at reform, a new accommodation, reached between the state and the private media, guaranteed the long term political survival of the ruling party and the commercial success of Televisa.

Changing domestic broadcasting and foreign relations

Almost a decade later, as a result of the discussions over NAFTA, the Free Trade Agreement between the United States and Mexico, the 'undemocratic' relationship between the Mexican government and the media again came under examination and criticism. This time voices in the United States joined in the criticism. *The Christian Science Monitor* observed that Televisa favoured any nominee of the governing PRI, to the extent that opposition candidates are rarely seen and never heard on any Televisa station.[11] In the 1991 federal elections in Mexico, the opposition candidates were absent from TV screens, which were dominated by announcements for the government programme *Solidaridad* (Dabrowski 1992, 11). Another US observer remarked that for this 'complete loyalty to the PRI, the government allows Televisa to enjoy monopoly control of the Mexican media market, for which it pays no taxes. In exchange for what would be owed, the government is given TV and radio time for messages, which at times are indistinguishable from political commercials' (Seid 1993, 18). In a US Congressional hearing it was reported that the Mexican Government still had *de facto* control of the nation's media in the form of the influence of regulatory bodies, licensing, and government

---

11 In a rare public appearance in a 1988 political rally for Salinas, Azcárraga proclaimed: 'Somos miembros del PRI y siempre hemos pertenecido al PRI. No creemos en ninguna otra formula y como miembros del partido, haremos todo lo que podamos para garantizar que nuestro candidato triunfe.' [We are members of PRI and we also have been. We don't believe in any other formula, and as party members, we will do everything we can to guarantee that our candidate wins.] (Darling 1992, 14).

funding of advertising revenue and operating costs, as well as outright intimidation. (United States Congress,1992)

Perhaps because of this indirect control, the Mexican Government felt it no longer needed to hold on to its own broadcasting resources. In 1991, after almost 20 years of operation, the Mexican government announced the sale of 170 government television stations forming the Imevision network (Channel 7). The Channel 13 government-owned network was put up for sale in March 1992. Bidders for the two networks included a Mexican regional multi-media group in partnership with the US media companies Capital Cities/ABC and Paramount Communications, Fox Broadcasting and Turner Broadcasting along with Mexican partners. The bid was awarded to Televisión Azteca, owned by a 50-member investment consortium led by Ricardo Salinas Pleigo (no relation to President Salinas de Gortari). Ricardo Salinas identified himself as a firm ally of the Mexican Government, stating, 'I am not going to launch a Government-bashing TV channel.'[12] The sale of the media package to Azteca was widely viewed as a political deal. The two Azteca channels receive about 10 per cent of audiences and slightly less than 10 per cent of all ad revenue.

The changing relationship between the state and the media

Since 1990, reforms and internal changes have made the Mexican media more professional, freer of the government and more competitive. The government relinquished its control over newsprint, banned the practice of overtly paying for favourable news coverage, and ceased to pay for journalists' travel expenses during trips. The government continues to use its control of a significant advertising budget, and its ability to reward favoured journalists by providing them access to officials, to discourage unfavourable reports. And, there continues to be some self-censorship by the media. Journalists are also reluctant to undermine their access to government officials by criticising them too freely. Many media outlets depend heavily on government advertising and do not wish to prejudice such income.

To a surprising degree, both print and electronic media provided full coverage of the Chiapas uprising in January 1994. For example, a cable television network broadcast a lengthy interview of EZLN leader Subcomandante Marcos. A provincial radio station broadcast the peace talks between the EZLN and the government team live, despite government admonitions that it not do so. The EZLN also sought to control coverage of the talks, and barred two television networks—one Mexican and one American—from its press conferences, claiming the networks were biased in favour of the government.

Broadcasting and the 1994 presidential elections

In September 1993, as part of a general package of economic and political reforms, the Mexican Government directed the Federal Electoral Institute (IFE), a semi-autonomous institution set up to ensure that federal elections were conducted fairly, to give a certain amount of broadcasting time to each of the political parties.

---

12 Tim Golden, 'Bib Mexican Retailer Wins Bidding for State-Owned TV,' *The New York Times.* July 19, 1993, Sec. D., p. 1.

The time would be paid for by the state. The parties could buy a limited amount of additional time. In January, 1994, eight of the nine political parties signed an agreement for Peace, Democracy and Justice. The agreement stated that equal access to the media was a necessary pre-condition for fair elections. The three major parties also agreed to hold a televised debate for the first time in the history of Mexican elections. The debate would be carried live by Televisa

Despite these measures, media coverage of the elections was far from fair. The Mexican Academy of Human Rights (AMHR) carried out an exhaustive content analysis of television broadcasting during the election campaign. Their report looking at Televisa's flagship news programme *24 Hours* and Azteca's *Hechos* news programme between January and April, 1994 concluded that the two networks did not present the presidential candidates in an objective and balanced manner. Over the course of the four months studied, the PRI enjoyed an approximately three to one advantage in total air time over the other two parties. In terms of presidential candidates, the ratio jumped to a six to one advantage for Zedillo over Cárdenas and Fernandez. The PRI candidate was also more likely to be portrayed with his own voice and image, at the top spot of the news broadcast.[13]

Sources of change: international expansion?

It seems highly unlikely that without a significant change in the Mexican political system, any real challenge will come to the Mexican private broadcasting media monopoly from within the country. Some competition to Televisa, however, may come from abroad. Paradoxically, these challenges to the domestic media monopolies may come from foreign, mainly US companies that can provide programming for potential rivals to giants like Televisa. The ability to buy programming from the United States with minimum costs for original programming, for example, allowed Multivisión, a Mexico City cable company not owned by Televisa, to create a 15-channel cable network serving 250,000 subscribers (Darling 1993).[14] The foreign investors in the Mexican media markets, however, in addition to being unlikely to want to challenge their host country's ruling party, will have to compete with a Mexican broadcasting industry that is fast becoming a transnational.

In 1976 Televisa exported approximately 12,000 hours of television programming and transmitted via satellite and microwave relays to its Spanish International Network, SIN, in the United States (de Noriega and Leach 1979). There were over 200 SIN affiliates in 1982 reaching 70 per cent of the US Hispanic population. Sixty-five per cent of SIN's programming came from Televisa. Ten years later, SIN affiliated over 400 stations in the United States including cable and UHF sys-

---

13 Mexican Academy of Human Rights in collaboration with Civic Alliance/Observation 1994. *The Media and the 1994 Federal Elections in Mexico: A Content Analysis of Television News Coverage of the Political Parties and Presidential Candidates.*

14 Cable television has been slow to develop in Mexico. Multivisión is the largest cable system, using MMDS, it had 300,000 subscribers by the end of 1993. It transmits Tele Uno and Cine Chanal and USA Networks, and is programming four of its own channels, plus three pay-per-view channels. Multivisión is affiliated with about 109 smaller cable companies in the interior of the country. The second cable system is Cablevisión, part of the Televisa group. (The US company TCI has 49 per cent stake in Cablevision) with 220,000 subscribers in Mexico City, carrying 22 channels. There are smaller cable systems throughout the country: Visión por Cable de Sinaloa, TV Comunal de Mexico, Visión por Cable de Sonora, TV Cable de Privincia, Telecale de Morelos, and TV Uruapan-Michoacan.

tems. Its gross earnings were $66 million, of a total Hispanic television advertising revenue in the United States of between $100 and $185 million.[15]

In 1988, as a result of a US court's decision against the Mexican owners in a case brought against them by their US associates charging foreign control, the SIN stations were sold to Hallmark Cards and First Chicago Venture Capital for about $300 million. The SIN network, its name changed to Univision, was sold to Hallmark a year later. Televisa retained its other companies in the US Hispanic market: Galavision, an Hispanic cable system; Protele for US and international TV sales; DATEL for telemarketing; Videovisa for the production and marketing of videocassettes; Fonovisa for the production and marketing of Spanish-language records; and ECO, a Spanish-language news service. Televisa remained the world's largest producer of soap operas for the two Spanish-language television networks in the United States, Univision and Telemundo, and produced about 7,000 hours of new programming annually for its four domestic channels, 70 per cent of which was exported (*Variety* 1987, 105).

In January 1993, the Federal Communications Commission approved the purchase by Televisa of 50 per cent of PanAmSat, valued at about $500 million. Panamsat, the main private satellite system serving Latin America, launched a second satellite for coverage of the Asia-Pacific region in the spring of 1994. Also in January 1993, Televisa returned as a minority partner in Univision, its former company, now composed of nine wholly owned US television stations, 29 affiliates, and over 600 cable affiliates reaching about 90 per cent of US Hispanic households. Televisa's partners[16] in Univision are the Cisneros groups from Venezuela and Jerold Perenchio, a US businessman.

The sale of Univision back to Televisa drew cries of 'cultural imperialism' from the United States. Within one month of taking over the new owners of Univision cancelled three US-produced programmes and fired seventy people who worked on them. Univision officials said the move was simply a response to ratings, not the implementation of what their critics fear will be a policy of abandoning the network's 50-50 balance between US and Latin American programming in favour of the cheaper imports (Puig 1993, B9).

Televisa is also expanding in Latin America. In 1992 Televisa purchased a 49 per cent share of Megavisión, a private commercial television channel in Chile, for $7 million and a 76 per cent share of the Peruvian television network, Companía Peruana de Radiodifusión (Channel 4) which owns ten TV stations and is affiliated with five others. Televisa has invested in a television production facility with the state-owned television channel in Argentina. In addition, Televisa acquired the Latin American and US enterprises of the American Publishing Group for $130 million, making it the world's largest publisher of Spanish-language magazines, with a total circulation of over 120 million copies, and set up a co-venture with Discovery Channel for Latin America.

---

15. *The Economist*, 16 May 1987, 67-8.

16 Because US law prohibits foreign companies from owning more than a 25 per cent interest in a broadcast television station, the investors will split Univision into two parts, the stations and the network. Perenchio will own 75 per cent of the station group, with the other partners sharing the remaining 25 per cent. Perenchio will also own 50 per cent of the network, with the two partners splitting the other 50 per cent.

The internationalisation of the Televisa model in Latin America has opened a new cycle in the international relations of Latin American broadcasting. In this new cycle, rather than the US networks, Televisa, a strong domestic monopoly accustomed to a close relationship with a party that has controlled the Mexican state for almost three-quarters of the century, plays the predominant role. The Mexican political system, however, is changing, and the dominant role of PRI is facing its most serious challenge ever. Televisa, despite its strong international expansion, will experience the aftershocks of this domestic political change in the coming years.

4 *Brazil*

L ike Mexico, the principal factor in the development of national broadcasting in Brazil was the relationship that developed over the last forty or so years between the industry and the country's political rulers. The mutual benefits of this relationship and the enormous size of domestic markets explain why Mexico and Brazil today have the two largest, most monopolistic, and politically powerful broadcasting industries in the Western hemisphere. Brazil's authoritarian rulers worked closely first with private radio stations, which they censored and in part directly controlled, and later with commercial television, notably TV Globo, which they helped create and had no need to control. In Brazil, the state's coming to terms with television took place later than it did in Mexico. In Mexico this accommodation was the natural outgrowth of the radio broadcasters' ongoing relationship with Mexico's political leaders, dating from the 1940s. In Brazil, a mutually beneficial working arrangement between television broadcasters and the government was reached after 1964 under a military dictatorship and well into the development of commercial broadcasting.

US investors were active in the establishment of commercial radio in Brazil as well as in the rise of TV Globo. Although this foreign influence strengthened commercial broadcasting, the manner in which the Brazilian industry evolved was first and foremost the result of the domestic political accommodations between broadcasters and Brazil's authoritarian rulers. The Brazilian media eventually proved the stronger partner in this relationship, outlasting the military and successfully transferring their loyalty to a popular civilian regime that was in part their creation. As the Brazilian media became increasingly independent from the government for advertising and other subsidies, the media's vast power contributed to the election and, later, the impeachment of the first freely elected Brazilian president in over thirty years.

The early Brazilian media

The first Brazilian radio stations, formed in the 1920s, were not commercial, but amateur, experimental radio clubs, run by engineers and intellectuals. Educator Roquette Pinto and Henry Moritze, the director of the National Observatory, inaugurated a radio station in 1923 as a member-supported cultural and educational club. Other pioneer Brazilian radio stations adopted the form of associations or member-supported clubs. The government taxed these non-commercial stations and their audiences with fees on stations and receivers. Radio grew slowly under this system. Although stations sometimes used different forms of indirect commercial sponsorship for their programmes, advertising was not allowed until after 1932 when a law changed the definition of broadcasting to allow for commercial activity. Even after 1932, government regulations hampered radio's commercial expansion, especially that of the smaller stations. Only the larger radio stations were able to comply with the complicated rules and obligations regulating their activities.

Despite their slow growth, Brazilian radio stations played a key role in the political events that changed the country in the early 1930s. By then radio was becoming an important vehicle for popular recording stars, sports events, comedy shows, news, and political debates. In 1929 Brazilian stations broadcast the election campaigns of Julio Prestes and Getulio Vargas. Radio Station Record of São Paulo played a prominent role in the Constitutionalist's Revolution of 1932 when student demonstrators seized its studios and aired a manifesto in favour of 'Liberty for Brazil and for the Constitution'. The broadcasts of Radio Record became a symbol of the political struggles of the population of São Paulo.

Brazilian radio shed most of its early cultural and educational roots over the first decades of its development. The country's push towards industrialisation and import substitution during the 1930s and 1940s stimulated the growth of commercial radio, popular entertainment, and mass advertising. Domestic and foreign advertisers and equipment salespeople recognised radio's potential to reach the growing Brazilian markets and fuelled radio's commercial expansion.

The Estado Novo

The Estado Novo of President Getulio Vargas (1937-1945) ruled Brazil during most of the initial commercial growth of radio broadcasting. Vargas had come to power in a *coup d'etât* in 1937. He ruled the country with dictatorial powers, using radio to facilitate his political objectives. In 1939 Vargas set up the Department of Information and Press (DIP) under the presidency in charge of government information and the media. Until the end of World War II, the DIP kept the Brazilian newspapers and radio stations, as well as theatre, books, films, and other cultural events under their tight political control.[1] The activities of DIP, especially in relation to radio broadcasting, had the dual purposes of controlling information, news, and public opinion; and promoting Brazilian culture, morals, and values. The National Radio of Brazil, Radio Nacional, already the leading radio in Rio de Janeiro, was taken over by the Vargas government in 1940 and, in 1942, it began nationwide shortwave broadcasts. Under Vargas, Radio Nacional received state financing to purchase the latest equipment and provide professional training for its staff. Using music and humourous programmes combined with government propaganda and information programmes like *Hora do Brasil*, the powerful shortwave facilities of Radio Nacional 'integrated' the enormous, culturally disperse nation and helped imbue it with a national identity. In addition to its own direct trans-

---

1 Much of the information on radio under Vargas is based on (Moreira 1992).

missions, daily broadcasts of *Hora do Brasil* were obligatory for all Brazilian radio stations between 8:00 and 9:00 pm. Radio Nacional co-produced radio programmes with US radio networks CBS, NBC, and the Mutual Broadcasting System under a programme promoted by Roosevelt's Good Neighbour policy.[2]

Despite Vargas' authoritarian control of radio through direct ownership and political censorship – in a six months period between December 1942 and August 1943 DIP reported 2,256 incidents of censorship of the words of songs and 1,088 incidents of censorship of recordings of radio programmes – there was little regulation of the commercial operations of the new broadcasting technologies (Moreira 1992). For many years the only law governing commercial radio was Decree 20,047, which became law in 1931, enacted almost ten years after the appearance of the first Brazilian radio stations. The Decree gave the state the right to regulate broadcasting services considered in the national interest. In 1932, Decree 21,111 set up a broadcasting licensing procedure that defined the rights and responsibilities of license holders (Federico 1982).

Many new commercial radio stations began in the 1940s, often in association with national newspapers chains. By 1938 the radio network of Assis Chateaubriand, Diarios e Emmissoras Associadas, already owned five radio stations, twelve newspapers, and a magazine. In the early 1940s, the Carvalho group set up the Radio Bandeirantes network, and the owner of the Globo newspaper, Roberto Marinho, founded Radio Globo. A hundred and ten radio stations were reported in operation throughout the national territory in 1944 (Federico 1982).

The introduction of television

In the 1950s owners of the Brazilian commercial radio stations and newspapers turned their attention to television. Assis Chateaubriand set up the first television stations, TV-Tupi, in São Paulo in 1950, and in 1951, TV-Tupi/Rio.[3] Soon after, TV-Paulista and TV-Continental began broadcasting in São Paulo and Rio de Janeiro. In 1953, Raul Machado de Carvalho inaugurated TV Record and the network Rede de Emmissoras Independentes REI. A year later, REI added TV Excelsior and TV Rio, two pioneering stations in modern Brazilian television programming and marketing techniques. Brazilian television was not limited to the wealthy, densely populated coastal cities. Before long, Brasilia, the new federal capital, had two television channels, and, in 1956, TV-Italcolomi went on the air in Belo Horizonte, also in the interior of the country (Federico 1982). There were only 200 television sets in Brazil at the time of the first transmission in 1950. Fifteen years later, in 1965, Brazil had a television audience of three million households and a highly competitive national television market.

The government distributed the first Brazilian television licenses without any preconceived technical plan and often in return for political favours. This was especially the case of many of the licenses distributed between 1956 and 1961

---

2 During this same period, a daily newscast called 'Reporter Esso,' based on news about World War II, was sponsored by Esso Standard Oil and distributed by the United Press. It was aired on many Brazilian radio stations.

3 In 1952 TV-Tupi/Rio began broadcasts of the Reporter Esso, the successful radio news programme. The broadcasts used newsreels from United Press International and CBS and were sponsored by Esso. The news programme remained on the air for almost 20 years.

during the administration of President Juscelino Kubitschek. Before the 1988 Constitution, the distribution of radio and television licenses was the exclusive prerogative of the President of the Republic. A 1990 survey by the magazine *Veja* found that around 20 per cent of Brazilian congressmen

> ... 'hold simultaneously the quickest and most efficient instrument for appearing before their electorate – a radio station, a television station or both. To this figure should be added a large number of politicians who, in one form or another, are the true owners of a broadcasting station, but employ the standard trick of leaving it in the care of family members or trusted friends.'[4]

More (1,250) radio and television station licenses were distributed during the administration of President José Sarney than during any previous presidential period.[5]

State-subsidised commercial broadcasting

The authoritarian regime of Vargas and the strict government control of information and the press after 1946 left a strong negative sentiment in the country against state intervention in radio and the press. With the return of democratically elected regimes in the mid-1950s, the private sector and the country as a whole were reluctant for the Brazilian state to take a major role in the administration of television. A liberal philosophy of private ownership and free competition prevailed. The government, however, controlled broadcast licensing and had considerable, although indirect, influence on the media through the distribution of the government advertising budget and the allocation of credits and loans for the private communication industries.

The Brazilian private broadcasters pushed for legislation that would guarantee the stability and growth of their commercial enterprises in the often unstable Brazilian political and economic climate. In 1953, Senator Marcondes Filho presented a bill for a national broadcasting code, based on the industrial code that had been adopted that same year. The code would eliminate all government control over the national radio and television system (Mattos 1982). In 1962, a Brazilian

---

4 'Cartorios Eletronicos, Electronic Registries,' *Veja*, July 25,

5 Distribution of Radio and Television Licenses.

Presidents	Administration	Radio Licenses	TV Licenses
Juscelino Kubitschek	1956-1960	–	14(1)
Janio Quadros	1960-1961	–	–
Joao Goulart	1961-1964	–	–
Castello Branco	1964-1967	–	23(2)
Costa e Silva	1967-1969	–	–
Emilio Medici	1969-1974	–	20
Ernesto Geisel	1974-1979	303	47
Joao Figueiredo	1979-1985	614	46
Jose Sarney	1985-1990	1,160	90
Fernando C. Mello	1990-1992	–	–

Until October 1992, the Collor de Mello administration had not granted any radio or television station licenses as it was waiting for the complementary laws to the 1988 Constitution. With the impeachment bill and the attempt to get the votes necessary to override it, the Collar administration sent National Congress 18 requests for radio and television stations licenses and 162 requests for the renewal of the station licenses. Sources:*Sergio Mattos, 1990, *Veja*, 1990 and *Estado de São Paulo*, 1992.

Telecommunications Code giving the private broadcasters the licensing guarantees they wanted was finally ratified in Law 4117. The telecommunication Code barred any contractual arrangements between the Brazilian private media and foreign capital and centralised the administration of the country's telecommunication services under the federal government.

The 1962 Telecommunications Code placed all the telephone services that had previously been provided independently by the different municipalities under the control of the federal government. Within the new system, each state telephone company formed part of the federal holding company, Telebras. In order to finance the expansion of the national telecommunications infrastructure, the code set up a national telecommunications fund and levied a 30 per cent tax on all communication services. The unification of the telephone system and the expansion of the national infrastructure indirectly subsidised the development of Brazilian commercial broadcasting. The public sector provided the necessary telecommunications infrastructure for the nationwide expansion of the television networks. The government also distributed investment credits and allocated a large percentage of the state advertising budget to the privately owned media.

The commercial consolidation of Brazilian television

The TV Tupi network of Diarios Associados, the first Brazilian television company, prospered through the early 1960s. The media conglomerate was composed of the newspapers *O Jornal do Rio de Janeiro* and 30 other newspapers. Diarios Associados owned a chain of 18 television channels, 36 radio stations, a news agency, an advertising agency, a public relations firm, and several of Brazil's leading magazines including *O Cruziero*, a Brazilian Life-type format and, until 1967 Latin America's largest selling magazine (Mattos 1982). The Diarios Associados conglomerate was under the direction of Joao Salom, who also served as president of the Brazilian Association of Radio and TV Enterprises, ABERT.

As the Brazilian television industry grew, its role in the general political and economic context of the country changed. Brazilian television discarded its highbrow programming of the past and reached out to attract the large mass urban audiences and the advertisers they brought with them. The Brazilian channels changed their earlier cultural programming to include more imported series, sports events, and national musical entertainment in order to attract audiences and bring in a larger portion of the nation's advertising budget.

Brazil's rapid industrial growth expanded the size of domestic markets and the purchasing power of important sectors of the Brazilian population. Others, however, found themselves trapped in the growing cities with shrinking incomes. The urban poor threatened political stability with demands for higher wages and political participation. In response to the growing unrest, in 1964 the military, backed in part by the right-wing political parties, seized control of the government.

TV Globo

TV Globo, the Brazilian television network that attained the greatest success of all national media enterprises, was established relatively late in the history of Brazilian television. When TV Globo's Channel 4 went on the air in Rio de Janeiro in 1965, the other networks had already consolidated their position in the national market, and fifteen years had elapsed since the first Brazilian television transmission. TV Globo's Channel 4 was part of Roberto Marinho's growing newspaper and radio conglomerate. In 1962, before putting the new channel on the air, Marinho had signed an approximately $5 million contract with Time-Life for the operation of TV Globo. The influx of foreign capital, technology, administrative experience, and programming the agreement brought allowed Marinho to begin transmission in 1965 with a new style and image of television. Instead of the often obsolete equipment and informal administration of some of the early Brazilian channels, TV Globo began as a modern television industry with all the latest creative, administrative, and technical advances. The foreign capital allowed TV Globo greater freedom of action in its choices of programming and management. Other channels like TV-Tupi soon found themselves losing audiences and advertisers to the modern TV Globo network.

The Time-Life investment in TV Globo was unconstitutional. The Brazilian Constitution and the National Telecommunications Code prohibited foreign investment in the mass media. The Brazilian military dictatorship that had come to power in 1964, however, did nothing to break Time's contract with Globo. Protests of unconstitutionality and unfair competition against TV Globo from the president of the Brazilian Broadcasters Association fell on deaf ears. In 1966 the Brazilian military rejected the unanimous condemnation of TV Globo by the Brazilian parliamentary commission set up to investigate the Time investment and allowed it to continue. The military saw Globo as a natural support to its regime. Globo's advanced technology, imported know-how, and quality mass productions gave the dictatorship an ideal communications system. In return, Globo's privileged financial position allowed the channel to take full advantage of the new regime's massive investments in national telecommunications infrastructure. The military's development policies of foreign investment and monopolistic concentration of the economy with state support to domestic industry fit well with the philosophy of Globo enterprises. As Amaral (1994, p. 26) observes:

> In many ways the military government continued a generalised and perverse national characteristic – the tendency towards financial and industrial concentration in the centre-south of the country, especially in São Paulo, and the resulting spread of a cartel system, resistant to orthodox anti-inflationary policies. In the case of the media, and particularly television, a meeting of minds appears to have occurred between Delfin Neto's (minister of finance under presidents Costa e Silva and Medici and administrator during the 'economic miracle') proclivity towards concentration and the military's obsession with national integration, which they thought would be facilitated through Embratel (The Brazilian Telecommunication Corporation).

TV Globo was born with the 1964 military dictatorship. The next 20 years of Brazilian television was the history of TV Globo as part of the military's project of conservative modernisation of the country. The military's goals of national security, economic concentration, foreign investment, and the unification of a national market needed a nationwide, easily controlled medium for advertising and cultural integration, similar to what Vargas had found with Radio Nacional. TV Globo provided the answer, becoming both instrument and product of the military regime. TV Globo was one of the military's main allies for the implementation of its politically, economically, and ideologically authoritarian model. At the same time, Brazilian television was one of the most notable products of the military's massive investments in modern communication technologies and its construction of a telecommunications infrastructure for the nationwide transmission of television signals.

Under the military Brazil's national product multiplied almost four times and the country grew to become the tenth largest industrial power in the world. Economic growth, however, was not equally distributed. In 1960, the poorest half of the Brazilian population received 17.4 per cent of the national product. By the end of the military's rule its share had dropped to 12.2 per cent. Between 1964 and 1984 the Gross National Product per capital almost doubled. The purchasing power of the minimum wage, however, fell by 51 per cent (Sachs 1985). Brazilian commercial television was the image and voice of the military regime controlling the country under these potentially explosive economic and political conditions. The sophisticated centralised industry provided a multi-faceted society, torn by violence and social injustice, with a homogeneous, non-conflictive and stable image of the world and of itself. In order to soften the real picture of the country's situation, self censorship was exercised on TV news to such an extent that President Medici once made the following confession:

I feel happy every night with I turn the television on to watch the news. While the news reports strikes, agitations, attempted assassinations and conflicts in other parts of the world, Brazil marches on in peace in the direction of development. It is like taking a tranquilliser after a hard day's work (Mattos 1992, 12).

Under the limited political discussion permitted by the military, it was inconceivable for Brazilian television to become the target of demands for change of any organised social group or political movement. Any change in the way the industry operated came from the state. An increase in national content in television during the military years, for example, was the result of state support for its goal of national culture. National programming was financed by credits from state banks, fiscal exemptions, coproductions with official organisations, and government advertising. The technological revolution of Brazilian television was facilitated by enormous state investments in telecommunications infrastructure and the creation of a large domestic and transnational advertising industry.

TV Globo's programming strategy of low-cost popular programmes and its political favour with the dictatorship made it the main beneficiary of the growth of Brazilian television. The military's 1968 investment in a national microwave relay system and in satellite reception and transmission facilities facilitated the rapid national expansion of the Globo network. TV Globo's 5-year agreement with Time-Life brought Globo the capital, technology, and administrative expertise necessary to gain ascendancy over the existing TV stations. TV Globo became the fourth largest television network in the world. Its enterprises covered a full range of production, distribution, and sales of radio, TV, newspapers, magazines, records, films, and video. The backbone of TV Globo was the soap opera – 'a national institute as potent as soccer, as popular as sex, as germane as daily life' (Variety 1987, 47).

Globo adopted a comprehensive programming strategy for its network with a national news programme and a series of domestic and imported soap operas. The strategy succeeded in attracting large audiences away from the existing channels. By 1970, the TV Globo channels in Rio de Janeiro and São Paulo had over 54 and 43 per cent of their respective television audiences (Potsch 1983). The older television network, TV Excelsior, once powerful under President Joao Goulart (1961-1964), lost its license in 1970, having slowly declined in audience popularity in relations to TV Globo. TV-Tupi, the first Brazilian station, hung on longer, but finally went bankrupt in 1980. The military distributed the cancelled channels between the media groups of Silvio Santos and Adolfo Bloch.

Between 1970 and 1980 the three original TV Globo channels grew to a national network of 46 affiliates. By 1982 Globo reached 99 per cent of the Brazilian households with TV receivers – approximately 15 million in a country of slightly over 112 million inhabitants. Globo's audience share at peak hours between 8:00 and 10:00 often reached 75 per cent of the population (Siqueira Bolano 1986). By 1980, in addition to television, the Globo enterprises (Radio Globo, Radio Eldorado, Radio Mundial and CBN) comprised the original newspaper *O Globo*, founded in 1925, the Globo radio network, established in 1944, a publishing house, a recording company, a video tape production company, an electronics industry, an art gallery, a theatre production company, and its own cultural foundation named after Globo president Roberto Marinho. Today, Globo owns two subscription television networks in Rio and São Paulo and is associated with groups elsewhere. Globo has grown into a financial conglomerate with branches in insurance (Seguradora Roma), banking (Banco ABC Roma, Corretora ABC Roma, Distribuidora ABC), agriculture, the food industry, real estate, mining (Compasa, Cobem and Manati), medical-care associations, electronic and the telecommunications industry (NEC do Brasil, Nectom and Victori Comunicações).

Other TV Networks

Although by far the largest, TV Globo was not the only private commercial TV network operating in Brazil. TV Bandeirantes forms part of the enterprises of Joao Saad, who operated commercial radio stations since the 1940s. In addition to eighteen radio stations, a recording company, and a record manufacturer, Bandeirantes has twenty-two affiliated television stations. At the early 1980s, two other networks came on the scene that were important to the development of the Brazilian television system. The government granted VHF licenses to the Sistema Brasileiro de Televisâo (SBT) in 1981 (which became the second largest national network), and to Rede Manchete (RM) in 1983. (presently in fourth place).

In 1981 the Brazilian Ministry of Communication and Information reported a total of 103 TV stations in the country: 42 Globo, 20 Bandeirantes, and 17 SBT.

Fifteen channels were classified as other, and nine were educational channels. Of the three Brazilian networks, however, Globo, with its sophisticated systems of audience research, marketing and production, was far in the lead, as is shown in the following table.

TV Networks: Audience Share in Brazilian Capitals (Percentage)

Capitals	Globo	SBT	Machete	Bandeirantes	Others
SP	57	22	4	6	11
RJ	73	9	6	7	5
POA	65	23	4	8	–
BH	71	22	4	3	–
CUR	67	24	3	3	3
REC	71	22	5	2	–
SAL	77	17	3	3	–
Bra	71	23	3	3	–

Source: *Mídia Dados 1993* (IBOPE, October 92, 8 Main Markets, 6:00 PM to 12:00 midnight).

The growth of advertising

The 1970s was the decade of the Brazilian economic miracle and of the growth of mass adverting. Brazilians acquired a new image of themselves as first and foremost consumers and of their country as a dynamic part of the world economy. This transformation, basically the job of advertising, was not cheap. In 1970 Brazil invested $350 million in advertising. By 1979 advertising had grown to $1.5 billion and accounted for 1 per cent of the Brazilian gross national product. Much of Brazilian advertising was controlled by agencies with significant foreign capital. Between 1971 and 1980 slightly under half the capital of the ten largest agencies was foreign. The firms that advertised their products on Brazilian television were also largely foreign-owned. In 1980, slightly less than a quarter of the advertisers were national, and, of these, a third were state-owned. The rest were transnational enterprises (Siqueira 1986).

The Brazilian government was a major advertiser. The state government of São Paulo became the largest advertiser in the local media, followed closely by the federal government. TV Globo accounted for 35 per cent of the total advertising in the country in 1978, including 85 per cent of television advertising of the ten largest agencies (Federico 1982).

National broadcasting policies

The Brazilian broadcasting laws predated the military regime. The Brazilian Telecommunications Code, enacted in 1962, combined the authoritarianism of the earlier Vargas regime, like the exclusive power of the president to distribute broadcasting licenses, with the liberal economics of the civilian governments that followed. The 1962 code was compatible with the centralisation later imposed by the military. Between 1965 and 1978, the powers the code gave the executive office enabled the military government to distribute almost 60 per cent of the television channels in the country to its supporters (Caparelli 1986). The code contained few

limitations on the activities of the private broadcasters, except restrictions on foreign and multiple ownership. These restrictions, however, were blatantly and openly violated by the military who, disregarding the verdict of a parliamentary
commission, refused to apply them to the Time-Life investment in TV Globo.

Under the framework of a new constitution and basing themselves on the 1962
telecommunications code, in 1967 the military set up a National Ministry of
Communications, the highest authority for all aspects of communications planning
and programmes. The national telecommunications system, established under the
ministry, included a National Telecommunications Council and its implementing
agency the National Telecommunications Department CONTEL/DENTEL; the
Brazilian telecommunications companies EC, Radiobras, and Telebras, that included Embratel, and its subsidiaries; and the National Telecommunications Fund,
FNT (Maculan, 1981). The military set aside non-commercial channels throughout the country for educational use. The educational television network, however,
did not begin operations until 1974 (Federico 1982).

The military's telecommunications projects included the expansion and modernisation of the urban, rural, and intercity telephone system; the establishment of
telex and data transmissions systems; and new international communication systems via underwater cable and microwave relays. Brazil's integration in INTEL-
SAT linked the country to worldwide satellites. The military made satellite
channels available to Globo and the Bandeirantes commercial television networks.
Later, the government put up its own national satellite system.

Through these and other measures the military consolidated the state's economic and technological leadership role in telecommunications. At the same time,
the regime created the conditions for the monopolistic expansion of the private
national communications industries through a policy of subsidies, technology
transfer, and joint ownership in association with selected transnational enterprises.
In a further measure of support to the private sector, the government constructed
a duty-free industrial zone for the electronics industry in Manaus deep in the
Amazon region. In 1980, the zone manufactured 85 per cent of the colour television sets sold in the country (Mattelart and Schmucler 1983).

During the military regime telecommunications were among the fastest growing sectors of the Brazilian economy.[6] As in the rest of the Brazilian economy, foreign investment was high in the electronics and communications industries.
Between 1970 and 1977 the communications sector accounted for 10 per cent of
the total amount of foreign capital invested in Brazil (Federico 1982).

Brazilian television and especially TV Globo grew with all the advantages
offered the private sector by the Brazilian military regime. The expansion of the
Globo national network and the objectives of national integration and security of
the Brazilian military were one and the same. Globo stretched over the entire territory, bringing Brazilians sophisticated pictures in brilliant colours and complex
imagery. Globo blended sports, patriotism, national news, and soap operas with
dexterous skill, the latest technology, and seemingly limitless funds. In a decade in

6   The Brazilian telecommunications industries expanded at a rate of 12 per cent in 1970, 18 per cent in 1971, 24 per
    cent in 1972, 30 per cent in 1973, 20 per cent in 1974, 15 per cent in 1975, and 20 per cent in 1976. The indus-
    try's contribution to the Gross National Produce grew from 1.7 per cent in 1970 to 3 per cent in 1975 (Federico
    1982).

which the Brazilian people had no organised representative political institutions and little right to free expression, TV Globo brought them an identity and gave them a dream.

Role of television in the transition to democracy

Between 1979 and 1985 under the Figueiredo administration the Brazilian economy began to show signs of exhaustion. By the end of his term, inflation had reached 200 per cent, and recessive measures had increased unemployment. Brazil's foreign debt was close to $100 billion. Sectors of business and industry began to disassociate themselves from the military regime, and previously docile politicians became rebellious. In the 1982 legislative elections the opposition won control of the state governments of São Paulo, Rio de Janeiro, Minas Gerais and Paraná, along with many seats in the House of Deputies. In the face of these defeats, the military announced they would not allow direct presidential elections to be held in the country until 1990. The moderate left-wing and centre political parties, however, supported a campaign for immediate and direct presidential elections.[7] The campaign for direct presidential elections was a widespread movement to pressure Parliament – where the military supporters held a majority – to approve a constitutional amendment allowing the president to be elected by direct popular vote. The catalytic role played by the Brazilian mass media in the campaign contributed an unexpected element in the movement.

Although all the domestic media eventually supported the campaign for direct presidential elections, TV Globo, although highly indebted to the military regime for its success, helped establish the national dimension of the anti-government movement by broadcasting the enormous demonstrations of over a million people that took place in Rio de Janeiro and São Paulo. In the final months of the military's power, the radical and unexpected changes in the Brazilian mass media and especially television were most striking in the Globo system.

The campaign for direct presidential elections consisted of rallies and demonstrations held in the first half of 1984 in all the state capitals and large cities all over Brazil. Broadcasters at first ignored the protests, and, until May, provided uneven coverage of the events. By June, however, they were unanimous in their enthusiastic and astute coverage of the campaign. The TV Globo network, for example, covered the rallies from noon on, in this way encouraging people who were still at home to come out and join the crowds.

The military never dreamed it would lose the support of the network that had been its semi-official mouthpiece and one of the principal beneficiaries of the Brazilian economic miracle. Public opinion, however, sensed that TV Globo was changing sides and the dictatorship was coming to an end. TV Globo was born with the regime and had grown strong with the regime, but it would not go down with the regime. Although the move for direct elections was ultimately not successful, the military's candidate was defeated later that year in the presidential elections held indirectly within the electoral college.

The mass media and especially TV Globo played a decisive role in this defeat.

---

7 Under the dictatorship, the president was chosen by an Electorial College, composed of members of parliament and representatives of the state legislative assemblies. For twenty years they had always chosen a general.

In the campaign for direct presidential elections, TV Globo at first had been caught off guard by the unexpected strength of public opinion against the military. In the campaign of opposition candidate Tancredo Neves in the electoral college, TV Globo took the initiative, helping to form public opinion and influencing the political process as the mouthpiece of the coalition movement of the Democratic Alliance.

On 15 January 1985 all the Brazilian radio and TV stations transmitted live broadcasts of Neves' election by voice vote in the electoral college. After his election and during the transition, TV Globo kept its distance from the military regime with a neutral and seemly objective coverage of the national news that had begun with the coverage of the campaign for direct elections. When Neves became ill and died before he could take office, TV Globo played a key role in legitimising his legal successor. Concerning this role, Brazilian analysts Guimaraes and Amaral (1988, 137), observe:

> The mass media and especially TV Globo had given legitimacy to the new regime. At the same time, TV Globo has assured its own legitimacy in the eyes of public opinion. A new TV Globo was born with the New Republic. Its role under the dictatorship was forgotten ... .The new leaders of Brazil had the media to thank for many things. However, they would now have to deal with the powerful new independent political force.

The power of this independent political (and economic[8]) force was demonstrated in the 1989 presidential elections in which Globo TV's preferred candidate, Fernando Collor de Melo, was the easy winner. A recent study of the 1989 Brazilian presidential elections (da Lima 1992) argues that the reasons for Fernando Collor's success in the 1989 elections can be found in the 'political scenario of representation' that was constructed in and by the media, especially television, and specifically by Globo's support for his candidacy.[9] Globo TV's news and ubiquitous soap operas called on the country to unite to support Collor, who was represented as a modern, optimistic outsider. In addition, Globo's coverage of Collor's opponent, Ignacio 'Lula' Silva, for example, in the presidential debates, made him look like a dangerous fool.

The power of Globo in the 1989 elections had made clear the need to 'democratise' the Brazilian media. The Brazilian Constitution of 1988 had provided some instruments for these changes, including the prohibition of monopolies or oligopolies in the media, the balance of public, private and state broadcasting systems, and the regionalisation of cultural, artistic, and journalistic productions. Few of these measures, however, were ever enforced, and the Collor administration for the most part dismantled any state-aid in the area of culture, especially to the Brazilian

---

8   The Brazilian economy invests about 2 billion dollars a year in advertising, 55 per cent of this to television, 30 per cent to newspapers and only 4 per cent to radio. TV Globo captures 70 per cent of television advertising. At prime time, 73 per cent of those watching TV choose Globo over the other six networks.

9   Collor had strong links with Globo since 1978 when he became president of his father's regional media empire, the Arnon de Mello Organisation, which is the biggest multimedia group in Alagoas, controlling the major state newspaper, *A Gazeta de Alagoas*, thirteen radio stations and TV Gazeta, an affiliate of the Globo TV network. Collor's brother was for several years regional director of Globo TV in Recife and São Paulo. Marinho [president of Globo] himself was a partner with Collor's father, with whom he bought the property on which the first Globo TV building was built in Rio de Janeiro (Lima 1992).

film industry and other cultural productions, and reduced popular access to culture all over the country (Festa 1993, 7). The Constitution also confirmed the prolongation of the license period for TV-broadcasters for 15 years and made if very difficult to revoke an existing broadcast license.

The same Globo power that had worked in favour of Collor, however, also worked against him. *The Washington Post* pointed out that Brazilians knew their president was in serious trouble when the Globo television network started giving generous coverage to the street rallies calling for his impeachment on charges of corruption. And, when word got out that Roberto Marinho had held a meeting with Vice President Itamar Franco, next in line of succession, Brazilians knew Collor, who resigned as a result of the corruption charges on 29 September 1992, was finished (Preston 1992, C1).

By relying on the private commercial media for support, the authoritarian Brazilian regime created a potent force in the Brazilian media. Although this force played a key role in Brazil's faltering return to democracy, it remained largely outside the orbit of the newly representative institutions of Brazilian society. Furthermore, there appeared little chance that the broadcasting monopoly would change with the introduction in Brazil of new telecommunications technologies.

In the early 1990s, UHF television services developed in the large urban consumer centres of the southeast and south. The largest success went to MTV of Rede Abril de Televisâo, dedicated exclusively to youth-oriented music for an audience between 14 and 34 years. About half MTV's material is imported from the United States. It uses the most advanced technology, and is the first station to record and exhibit digital audiovisual signals. MTV started in São Paulo and has spread to 116 cities on broadcast and pay TV. It is owned by one of the country's largest publishing groups, Editora Abril. TV Jovem Pan was created to be the first UHF television. It is owned by two successful radio station in the city of São Paulo with a long tradition of news coverage: Jovem Pan 1 (AM, and Jovem Pan 2 FM). The stations, however, has limited commercial success.

Globosat of Rede Globo and TVA of the Editora Abril groups's Rede Abril de Televisâo are the main players in cable television. Both Globo and TVA began with scrambled over-the-air delivery systems, UHF for TVA and C-band satellite delivery for Globo. Now, major cities are being wired by Net Brasil, a Globo affiliate, TVA, and a third companies, Multichannel. In 1993 Globo's operation was divided into two separate offshoots. Globosat remained as the Rio-based programmer and Net Brasil was set up in São Paulo to handle the actual cabling. Globo has about 50 cable franchises throughout the country. Globosat uses four of Globo's own channels, Telecine, Top Sport, Globosat News (GNT) and Multishow, as well as programmes from ESPN, Tele-Uno, NBC News and Turner Broadcasting. Globo was the only network which has been granted a license for CATV systems. Globo also controls 57 per cent of cellular telephony of Brazil, thanks to the association of Brazilian NEC, owned by Roberto Marinho, with a Japanese firm. This company holds a monopoly for cellular telephony in São Paulo, Paraná, Bahia and Rio de Janeiro, the cream of the Brazilian market. Globo clearly made the transition to the new communication technologies as easily as it did to the new civilian government.

The growth of democracy, however, could also increase competition in the Brazilian media industries. Pay-TV will soon receive another boost as Communications Minister Sergio Motta, under newly elected Brazilian President Fernando Henrique Cardoso, awards another 100 'wireless cable' concessions. The minister announced that concessions will be grounded in merit and probably based on auctions. In previous years, concession usually went to members and friends of the Congress. This year it might be different. And, the ministry is drafting regulations to a new cable TV law, which will allow foreign investors to own up to 49 per cent of any system, adding yet another actor to the Brazilian broadcasting balance.

5 *Venezuela*

Venezuela's domestic broadcasting industry, like that of Mexico and Brazil, grew into a quasi-monopoly with strong international export activities. During the course of its development, Venezuelan broadcasting was bolstered by foreign investment and personnel from the United States and from Cuba. In contrast with both Mexico and Brazil, however, Venezuelan broadcasting, after an initial period of dictatorship, developed under a largely democratic system. After the fall of Venezuelan dictator Marcos Perez Jimenez in the late 1950s, democratically elected leaders of Venezuela were able to build a relationship with the private media that allowed for the largely unregulated development of commercial broadcasting.

The good relationship between the Venezuelan state and commercial broadcasters was broken temporarily in the 1970s in a confrontation that began during the first administration of President Carlos Andres Perez and lasted for almost a decade. The private sector emerged fortified from this confrontation, that took place between an elected democracy and a strong national industry. Another confrontation between the state and broadcasters occurred two decades later, in the early 1990s, following the abrupt termination of the second administration of President Perez. Those broadcasters who had been closely linked financially to the Perez administration emerged from this confrontation greatly weakened.

Today, although seriously affected by the almost total collapse of the banking and insurance industries and a shrinking domestic economy, Venezuela has the third largest television industry in Latin America, with an international expansion greater than that of Brazil. This strong international expansion, and the generalised discrediting of Venezuelan politicians and political parties[1] have contributed to the economic and, increasingly, the political autonomy of the Venezuelan media, despite the sharp decline of the Venezuelan economy.

Venezuela's late start

The 20th century did not begin in Venezuela until 1935, when the dictatorship of Juan Vicente Gomez ended. But that time, Mexico already had a prosperous private broadcasting industry, and radio in Argentine, Chile and Uruguay had enjoyed

---

1. Venezuelan President Carlos Andres Perez resigned in 1993 amid charges of corruption. President Jaime Lusinchi, (1984-1989) is also facing a criminal investigation.

at least a decade of commercial expansion under democratic rule. The long reign of General Juan Vicente Gomez, from 1908 to 1935, left a deep scar on the country. The brutal, able general cut short the civil wars, anarchy, and chaos that had plagued Venezuela since its independence, yet he ruled the country like a family farm. Gomez died in office in 1935, leaving behind a country with less than 2,000 university students, only four national newspapers, and a literacy of rate of 10 per cent. The generals that followed continued many of his same policies.

In 1945 a coalition of young politicians and military officers overthrew the military and set up a revolutionary junta headed by Romulo Betancourt. The revolutionary junta encouraged political participation and reformed the education system, the labour laws and the country's contacts with the foreign oil companies. In 1947 Venezuelan novelist Romulo Gallegos won the first free elections ever held in the country. Less than a year later a military coup overturned the Gallegos administration. The military ruled Venezuela for the next ten years, until 1958. Six of these years were under the rule of General Perez Jimenez.

Supported by the transnational petroleum companies and the Venezuelan upper classes, Perez Jimenez developed the country's infrastructure and set up some basic industries. Under these circumstances, commercial radio expanded as advertisers began to reach out to the growing urban markets. Oil revenues created an economic bonanza for the state and the elites. Perez Jimenez guaranteed peace and stability and undertook a series of grandiose public works, one of which was the introduction of television.

The introduction of television

With the first transmission of Televisora Nacional Channel 5 in November 1952 Venezuela became the ninth country in the world to have television. It was, in the words of Professor Antonio Pasquali, 'a useless, hasty gesture of a vain and wasteful dictatorship, attempting to re-establish the myth of modernisation, progress, and order'.[2] The military placed the new technology under the ministry of the interior. Venezuelan television went on the air eight days before the presidential elections of 1952 in which the military sought to legitimise the government of its candidate General Perez Jimenez. Within the next year the military had allowed two commercial television on the air – Televisa Channel 4 and Radio Caracas Television Channel 2, both transmitting without broadcasting licenses.[3]

Television under the new democracy

In 1957, General Perez Jimenez's attempt to remain in power through a referendum backfired. He had lost support, and the main political parties, the Church, the unions, peasants, and sectors of the armed forces rose up against the continuation

---

2   Personal interview with the author.

3   The Venezuelan Telecommunications Law of 1940 reserved all systems of communication exclusively for the use of the state. In 1941 the regulation of the Telecommunications Law opened up the possibility of licensing some communication services to private entities. In the case of television, however, licenses were limited to scientific and experimental purposes. Licenses to operate commercial TV channels could not be allocated before their services had been codified and regulated by the executive. This had not been accomplished by the time the commercial channels went on the air in 1953, and it never was.

of military rule. The dictator was forced to flee the country. Acción Democrática, the party of Romulo Betancourt, governed the country for the following ten years, gradually reforming Venezuela's social and political structure.

The new civilian leaders by and large ignored television. They had grown up with newspapers and the printed word and gave little importance to the new electronic technologies. Moreover, they were firm liberals. Press freedom and freedom of expression, especially from government censorship and repression, had been important demands in their struggle against the authoritarian regimes, and they were loath to increase state ownership of the media. Anyway, television, still reaching a small national audience, had little weight in national politics. In 1963 only 25 per cent of Venezuelan homes had a television set.

The relationship between the civilian government and the private media was good, and there was little need for government interference or censorship. The democratic governments were neither prepared for nor interested in formulating policies for private commercial broadcasting. The Venezuelan state had a few small broadcasting facilities of its own that had been established under the military, the original state-run radio and television station (Channel 5) and a small audiovisual unit operating within the ministry of education. During its ten years in power Acción Democrática felt little need to expand these resources any further.

After the fall of Perez Jimenez, Channel 5 had changed its propaganda role to one of culture and education. In 1961, for example, the channel had carried out a national literacy campaign, increasing its modest geographic coverage with a new transmitter and, in 1966, adding still another. Channel 5 never achieved national coverage or received sufficient funding to produce high quality national cultural programmes. Its content consisted mostly of recitals by local musicians, roundtable discussions and conferences, and films borrowed from foreign embassies and cultural missions.

The ten years of government by Acción Democrática, however, witnessed major changes in Venezuelan private commercial television. The three US TV networks all formed partnerships with a domestic station in the Venezuelan television market. In 1960 Televisa Channel 4 was purchased by the Cuban-Venezuelan industrialist Diego Cisneros, who changed the name to Venevisión. A major part of the stock (42.95 per cent) of Venevisión was acquired by ABC, in violation of the 1941 broadcasting regulation limiting foreign ownership of commercial broadcasting stations to 20 per cent. NBC already owned 20 per cent of Channel 2 Radio Caracas Televisión. In 1965 President Raul Leoni awarded a license to operate a new commercial TV channel, CVTV Channel 8, to the Vollmer industrial group in association with the exiled Cuban television owner Goar Mestre, Time-Life, and CBS.

Rafael Caldera, the leader of the opposition party, Partido Social Cristiano COPEI, was elected president of Venezuela in 1968. Caldera was the first Venezuelan president to regularly use the television medium. Television reached 45 per cent of Venezuelan households in 1969 and, by 1972, was receiving the same amount of advertising as newspapers. Caldera held weekly televised press conferences throughout his administration. Acción Democrática returned to power in 1973 with the overwhelming victory of Carlos Andres Perez. In the presidential elections of 1973, for the first time television played a key role in the political campaigns. A third of the total advertising expenditures for the year went to the presidential campaigns, much of this to television, now reaching about half the Venezuelan households.

A proposal for national communication policies

Venezuelan broadcasting had operated virtually without regulation since its inception. The principal broadcasting law dated from 1940. Much of the regulation on television was self-regulation on the part of broadcasters and advertisers. In 1964 commercial broadcasters had adopted a Code of Ethics for Venezuelan Television, containing guidelines for TV content. These guidelines were based on guidelines proposed by the Asociacion Interamericana de Radiodifusión (AIR), the Venezuelan Chamber of Broadcasters, the Venezuelan Federation of Advertising Agencies, and the National Association of Advertisers, all representatives of the private industry. In 1967 these national associations signed an agreement on television advertising stipulating a maximum limit of 12 minutes an hour for commercials plus two minutes for promotional material from the station (Agudo Freites 1976).

When President Carlos Andres Perez entered office, Venezuelan had been governed by democratically elected governments for 15 years. High prices for crude oil, the country's main export, gave the country of feeling of economic well-being and stability. The newly elected president had witnessed television's power in his campaign, where, for the first time, US consultants played key roles advising presidential candidates on the use of television. Once in office, President Perez turned his attention to the Venezuelan state's inadequate media resources and the lack of any public policy for national broadcasting. He was aided in his efforts domestically by the increased oil wealth of the country, much of which was now in state hands with the 1976 inauguration of Petroleos de Venezuela as the state-owned oil monopoly. Internationally, his efforts were backed by a growing Third World movement for media reform and a new world information and communication order, much of which was formulated by the member countries of the non-aligned movement, of which Venezuela was a leading member.

During the Perez administration, Venezuelan television reached about 50 per cent of the country's households. Economic growth had propelled huge increases in advertising and fuelled the expansion of multi-media ownership groups which had bought out many of the early pioneers of broadcasting. After the Cuban Revolution in 1959, Venezuela had become home to the Cuban private television industry, fleeing expropriation and the economic policies of Fidel Castro. Cuban capital entered the Venezuelan media, and Cuban managers, artists and directors filled positions in all the private Venezuelan TV channels.

Despite the Venezuelan media's commercial growth, until the late 1960s, television was not the subject of much policy discussion or debate. Occasional criticism of television, similar to that going on at the time in the United States on violence and children's programming, was usually confined to the universities. These studies bemoaned television's low intellectual and cultural level and deplored that the new technology was not put to better social use.[4] In general, how-

---

4 The first criticism of television came from the Central University of Caracas. In 1963, Antonio Pasquali, the former director of the school of journalism and the director of the Institute of Communication Research, published *Comunicación y Cultura de Masas*. Three years later, Pasquali wrote *El Aparato Singular*. Both books criticised tele-

ever, few scholars or political leaders suggested policies departing from the prevailing model of private commercial broadcasting.

The discussion of Venezuelan television, however, soon spread beyond the walls of the universities. The increased importance of television in the presidential campaigns was a factor in this spread. In 1973, for the first time television played a key role in the formation of public opinion and the electoral success of the presidential candidate. The political parties found themselves in the novel position of having to curry favour and form alliances with the private television channels in order to finance the high costs of television advertising (Capriles 1980). The growing political and economic influence of the television industry converged with the intellectuals' calls for the reform of its content. When they did, the owners and managers of Venezuelan television, marked by the experience of the Cuban Revolution and fortified by investments from the US television industry, were prepared to resist what they considered state intervention in broadcasting.

Carlos Andres Perez began his five-year term in office with an overwhelming electoral majority. He did not look much like a media reformer. Perez was hated by many for his role as interior minister under the previous administration in the repression of the guerrilla movements. He was considered a protégé of Romulo Betancourt and a representative of the most conservative and orthodox wing of Acción Democrática. His moderate, dynamic image during his presidential campaign, however, had attracted a large number of middle-class voters. Soon after taking office, the new administration proposed a flurry of new legislation aimed at significantly changing the Venezuelan economy and social structure, including the operations of the mass media.

Less than two weeks after assuming office, Perez issued a decree setting up a commission to organise a National Council of Culture, CONAC. The council would plan, coordinate and execute the cultural activities of the Venezuelan state. Within the first month of his presidency Perez reorganised the Central Office of Information (OCI) under the direction of the Minister of Information. OCI was put in charge of the budget and planning of all government information and advertising (ININCO 1977).

The government's sudden, unexpected interest in the management of its advertising budget caught the private sector by surprise. In the past the government, by far the largest advertiser in the country, had distributed its ample budget in a haphazard fashion through many different government offices. These offices often became small, independent pockets of influence, for the most part favouring the larger media, especially television. Eduardo Fernandez, the parliamentary leader of the opposition, expressed his concern over the implications of the new office,[5] and the secretary general of the Christian Democrats accused the new administration of

---

vision's excessive use of advertising and encouragement of consumption especially among lower income groups. In 1969, *La Televisión Venezolana y la formación de estereotipos en el niño*, by Eduardo Santoro fuelled the incipient discussion of the media. Santoro, a social psychologist at the Central University, studied the effects of television on Venezuelan children, concluding that television taught children about a world of greed and violence where culture, science, and technical advancement were given no importance. Also in the late 1960s, Marta Colomina de Rivera of the University of Zulia published *El Huesped Alienante: Un estudio sobre audiencia y efectos de las radio-telenovelas en Venezuela.* Her book on the psychological effects of soap operas on lower income women in urban slums concluded that it was useless to continue spending public funds on education without a significant change in the content of television.

5 *El Universal*, 19 April 1974.

turning the Central Office of Information into a gigantic instrument of totalitarian threats against political liberties.[6] Private media owners also expressed concern with the new president's attempts to increase government control of the media.[7]

In a speech delivered soon after taking office to the Inter American Association of Broadcasters (AIR), a powerful association of private broadcasters from throughout the region including the United States, Perez explained that it was impossible to regard broadcasting merely as entertainment, or simply as a creative vehicle. Broadcasting, Perez stated, is a public service, perhaps the most important public service of our time, and a public service that can do either great good or great harm (OIC 1976). In another speech before the Venezuelan Chamber of Broadcasters, Perez assured media owners that he was willing to allow radio and television to be exploited by private individuals for commercial purposes. But, he added, he felt the need to set up publicly owned media, which, he promised, would not compete with the private sector (Perez 1976).

Perez enjoyed wide popular support. Under extraordinary economic powers voted Perez by the Venezuelan Parliament, he introduced an avalanche of reform measures like the nationalisation of petroleum and the iron and steel industries. The high level of popular approval for the Perez administration made it hard for the private broadcasters to challenge his domestic and international media policies. The Perez administration's ratification of Decision 24 of the Andean Pact, a regional agreement like the European Economic Community with a strict code on foreign investment affecting services like banking and communications, had serious implications for the foreign investments of the Venezuelan broadcasters. Under Decision 24, no new foreign investment was allowed in television. Any foreign firm operating in Venezuela had to sell 80 per cent of its stock to national investors within three years of the agreement.

The purchase of Channel 8

In September 1974 the government announced it had successfully completed negotiations to purchase Channel 8, Cadena Venezolana de Television, which it was renaming Venezolana de Television. Channel 8 had been in economic difficulties for several years. It had invested heavily in new technologies to prepare to transmit in colour. The Venezuelan government paid $6 million for Channel 8, placing it under the Central Office of Information, along with the Venezuelan Telephone Company and the Venezuelan Development Corporation.

Soon after the government purchased Channel 8, the two remaining private channels insisted that it was incompatible with the dignity of the state to allow commercial advertising on its new channel. The private broadcasters demanded that the government continue to distribute its advertising budget equally between the two private channels. They were successful in their bid. Although Channel 8 did not accept commercial advertising, it continued to air programming, regularly interrupted with promotional and other government information. The amount of foreign TV content on Channel 8 increased under state ownership, reaching levels higher than those seen on the privately owned channels. This was mainly because

6 *El Universal*, 20 April 1974.

7 *El Universal*, 23 May 1974.

the state channel was never given the resources to produce its own programming. Channel 8's news content remained low, under 5 per cent. The government's management of Channel 8 and government advertising were indications of the contradictions between the rhetoric of the government's policies and their actual implementation. They also showed the beginnings of a new relationship being forged between the state and the private broadcasters (Alfonso 1985).

Some critics within Perez' administration felt it was foolish to antagonise the private media by expanding the state-owned broadcasting sector when their support was sorely needed for the administration's more important economic and political reforms. The private media soon took up their own defence, however, attacking the new state media policies as a manifestation of what they considered Perez's populist and statist tendencies. The RATELVE project became the main target of these attacks.

RATELVE

In November 1974 the commission named by Perez to organise the National Council of Culture set up a Committee on Radio and Television, RATELVE, with the task of preparing realistic and politically defendable national broadcasting policies. The committee, under the coordination of Antonio Pasquali, a university professor, represented a wide range of social sectors including the Church, the unions, and the armed forces, although it had no representative of the private sector. The private media's attacks on RATELVE were immediate and devastating, giving the project notoriety and an almost mythical power over the media long before RATELVE's policies were conceived or released to the public. As a result, the government took away its support for the initiative, partially to guarantee the success of other legislative programmes with higher priority.

RATELVE, a proposal for a new broadcasting policy for the Venezuelan government, defined seven general principles and presented an ideal model for broadcasting.[8]

The RATELVE report compared the stated aims of the existing institutions and organisations of broadcasting in Venezuela and their actual programmes and achievements. The comparison revealed a small, underfinanced public sector with little policy or planning capacity and slight impact on national broadcasting, and a vast, highly efficient commercial organisation with little concern for development

---

8 These principles were:

    a. Without communication there is no community, therefore, communication is by definition political.

    b. Social communications is not a branch of the cultural of the advertising industries; it cannot be reduced to purely a commercial dimension.

    c. Broadcasting is always and necessarily a public service even if it is partially and exceptionally given in concession to the private sector.

    d. Broadcasting is a fundamental instrument of development.

    e. Broadcasting must fulfil the needs and demands of the nation.

    f. The global direction of broadcasting is the task of the state, not as a monopoly but in harmony between the public and the private sectors.

    g. The essential tasks of the state are to harmonise the public and private broadcasting sectors, raise the level and maximise and diversify the coverage of public broadcasting, and implement a policy to finance the new public broadcasting services.

goals or wider social needs. The report proposed the general control of broadcasting by the state and the creation of a new organisation to develop a national public broadcasting system. Private broadcasting would compete with the public broadcasting sector under conditions of financial, technical, and geographic equality. Public sector broadcasting would be partially financed from a tax on television and radio receivers and advertising. This 'planned, complementary, and noncompetitive system' would provide the Venezuelan audience national coverage and maximum choice.

The private sector's unified and energetic opposition to the recommendations of RATELVE was the most obvious reason for the withdrawal of government support for the project. In the words of one member of the committee, Venezuelan media historian Hector Mujica, 'It was easier to nationalise the petroleum, aluminum and steel industries than to brush the private commercial broadcaster with a rose petal.'[9] There were, however, other reasons for RATELVE's failure, among them the lack of popular support for the new policies among the Venezuelan population. Despite Perez's popularity, the government management of Channel 8 gave the Venezuelan people little hope that anything significant would be gained with increased state management of the media. The administration made no effort to mobilise public opinion behind the measure. Another reason was the distrust of Perez by the members of the opposition political party, who felt that Perez would use the new state media for his own political purposes. While the RATELVE project languished in Parliament and eventually was forgotten, Perez turned his attention to the international discussion of media reform and a New World Information Order, a less controversial issue at home and one that only remotely affected the interests of the Venezuelan private sector.

The V National Plan and the National Council of Communication

In March 1976 the Perez administration released the V National Plan for 1976-1980. For the first time a national plan included social communication among the areas of social and economic development. The plan announced the establishment of a National System of Social Communication and of a Ministry of Information. None of these initiatives, however, was successful. Instead of the announced ministry of information, Perez eventually set up a ministry of information and tourism, based on the model of the Spanish Government, placing at its head an ex-governor of Caracas with experience in tourism and public opinion who had been Perez's advisor during his presidential campaign. The Perez administration continued to back international and regional initiatives for communication policies, like the Latin American Pool of National Information Systems and other UNESCO initiatives. The approaching presidential campaign, however, occupied the last year of the Perez administration, and no further mention was made of national policy changes affecting the media.

---

9 Personal interview with the author.

The Administration of Luis Herrera Campins (1979-1983)

Although the Social Democrat party of President Perez avoided the topic of the media during their campaign, this was not the case of the successful Christian Democrat challenger, Luis Herrera Campins. Campins, a former journalist, promised to put an end to the confusion that marked the relationship between the government and the media, increase the coverage and quality of public broadcasting, and consider setting up a participatory mechanism for broadcasting management with representatives of the government and of other social organisations (Alfonso 1985).

During the first years of his administration Campins kept the discussion of the media on the front burner, stressing the need for a national broadcasting policy that would give the state a role in the development of social communication and temper the commercial abuses of television. Campins' administration modified the structure of the ministry of information and tourism set up by Perez, established a planning committee for cultural development and social communication, and enacted laws regulating advertising and local programming. These included the prohibition of advertising of alcohol and tobacco and the establishment of certain categories of programming for children and women. Under Campins, the government Channel 8 was authorised to use commercial advertising. The authorisation was partially the result of growing deficits in the public budget and of the government's inability to finance the channel. It also came from the opposition-controlled parliament's refusal to authorise further public funding for a channel it felt was being used for political propaganda during an election year. As the Campins administration drew to a close and the presidential campaign began, the support of the private mass media became more essential, and further discussion of national media policies was dropped.

In 1984, Jaime Lusinchi, a Social Democrat, became president. With the foreign debt threatening economic stability and petroleum prices dropping, the new government needed all the support it could to administer the economic crisis. It was no time to stir up problems with the mass media, and any talk of expanding public media was abandoned. In 1989 Perez returned to power (Venezuelans presidents may serve more than one term but not consecutively). He campaigned on a promise to reduce the public sector. His second administration was marked by two attempted military coups, growing economic difficulties of the Venezuelan population, and charges of corruption and scandal. He resigned under a cloud of accusations of mismanagement in 1993. During the second Perez administration, between 1989 and 1993, the private media expanded greatly, often financed by government-insured loans from private banks, also owned by media owners. Banks and media groups acquired radio, television, cable and publishing assets throughout Venezuela, according to Sweeney (1995), often in violation of existing laws and regulations regarding the concentration of media ownership.

A dangerous thing happened during the second Perez administration. Banking and commercial groups with close personal ties to President Perez joined forces to acquire control of Venezuela's privately owned national and regional media, as part of a strategy to amass great economic wealth and political power in the 'new' Venezuela of open markets and trade liberalisation. The principal architects and/or beneficiaries of this strategy were the late Pedro Tinoco, whose position in the Central Bank presidency during the second Perez government was paralleled by a remarkable explosion in Banco Latino's growth and wealth. Other key players in this strategy were Gustavo and Ricardo Cisneros of the Organisation Diego Cisneros; and Jose Alvarez Stelling of the Banco Consolidado Group. Eugenio Mendoza of the now largely defunct Mendoza Group, and more distantly, Orlando Castro.[10]

According to Sweeney, President Perez openly supported his friends' strategy of acquiring media assets. He also indirectly encouraged sales of some media properties when he reneged on the pledges of earlier governments to honour the private sector's foreign debt obligations at subsidised exchange rates, forcing indebted media owners to sell, often to banks. As they acquired media properties, many of individuals close to Perez expanded their financial enterprises. Banco Latino became the largest financial group in Venezuela. Orlando Castro expanded his insurance and banking empire, purchasing Banco Republica. The political side of this arrangement was key. Banks would finance their candidates, while their media would sell these candidates to voters, in much the same way as occurs with Televisa in Mexico and Globo in Brazil. The political end of the arrangement, however, faltered with the two coup attempts against Perez, the scandals, and his resignation.

In the elections that followed Perez' resignation, 'outsider' Caldera was voted into power and proceeded to nationalise every single bank whose owners were close to President Perez. These financial institutions were poorly managed and often corrupt. They also owned substantial publishing and broadcasting assets, for example 40 radio stations in the case of Castro, which are now under government control. Under President Caldera, direct government ownership of the media as well as the power exercised through exchange rate policies, greatly increased the role of the Venezuelan state in the broadcasting sector.

Was Venezuelan broadcasting really different?

Venezuela's commercial broadcasting industry developed relatively late compared to industries in Mexico and Brazil. The Venezuelan anti-government political climate after the fall of the dictatorship in the 1950s converged with commercial interests to allow a largely unregulated television industry to emerge. By the time television had acquired sufficient strength as a medium to make it a powerful tool in elections, it was too late for the state to forge any relationship with broadcasting other than laissez-faire. In addition, Venezuela's strong 'internationalised' private sector managed by exiled Cuban broadcasting professionals and US investors fuelled Venezuelan television's long and deep opposition to state intervention. These factors converged to form a Venezuelan commercial broadcasting industry similar to that of Mexico and Brazil. Two large companies work closely together, controlling the vast majority of the country's broadcasting resources, while public broadcasting languished, and most popular movements are excluded from the media. A further concentration of the media and banking occurred under the second administration of Carlos Andres Perez that served to bring the media closer in

---

10 John Sweeney, 'Some Thoughts on the Venzuelan Media,' paper presented at the seminar on 'The Role of the Media in Venezuela: Is it a Stabilising or Destabilising Force?' SAIS, John Hopkins University, Washington D.C. March 6, 1995.

line with certain political interests and elites. The collapse of these interests left the Venezuelan state in the unlikely position of holding a significant number of media assets, which will most likely revert to private ownership.

The internationalisation of Venezuelan television

The two main commercial television network in Venezuela are Radio Caracas Television, owned by the Phelps/Granier family, and Venevisión, owned by the Cisneros family. Radio Caracas Television, RCTV, broadcasts on Channels 2, 3, 7 and 10 nationwide with a network of 20 stations. The Phelps family group which also owns an AM and an FM radio station in Caracas; *El Diario de Caracas*, a daily newspaper; Selevan, a publishing house; Mercalibros, a book distributor and Sonografica, a record company. Other media holdings of the Phelps Group include: Telearte production studios and equipment; Sonoartists Management of musical talent; Sono-International record distribution; Recordland chain of record and video sales; Cromapress printing; Videorama home video sales and rental services; and Fonotalent management of actors and other talent. The group also has its own record and cassette manufacturing companies.

Internationally, Radio Caracas Television owns Miami-based Coral Pictures Corporation, the largest purveyor of Latin American telenovelas in the world, selling programming produced by RCTV. Radio Caracas Television, along with the Buenos Aires cable network VCC, is a co-owner of Gems, a Latin American cable channel specialised in soap operas and other programmes designed to appeal to women. The channel transmits an eight-hour block, repeated twice a day, on Spacenet II and Intelsat satellites to all of North and Latin America.

The other national network, the Corporacion Venezolana de Televisión, Venevisión, belongs to the Diego Cisneros Organisation, ODC, that owns department stores, supermarket chains, soft drink and manufacturing plants, and several computer assembly and distribution concerns. It operates twenty-one stations through Channels 4, 6, 7, 9, and 12. In addition to Venevisión, the ODC owns a radio network, Radio Visión, with fifteen stations throughout the country; a record company, Sonorodven; a home video distributor, Videorodven; a publishing house, Circulo de Lectores; a company for handling and managing talent and live productions, Big Show Productions; and an advertising agency based in Miami, Medcom. ODC also owns Television Latina, based in Miami, for the sales and distribution of its television exports in the United States.

Internationally, Venezuela is also the home of HBO-Olé, a joint venture between HBO/Time-Life Warner and Venezuela's Ominivisión Latin Entertainment. With an uplink from Venezuela, HBO-Olé is carried by 130 cable operators from Mexico to Argentina. Olé operates out of the facilities of Ominvisión, a domestic pay-TV services in Venezuela.[11]

The relationship between the family media conglomerates and Venezuelan political leaders is complex. Political leaders and media owners belong to the same

---

11 Rafael Urbina, co-founder and former co-chairman of the HBO Olé service for Latin America is planning a new service, based in Florida, the first US-to-Europe DBS pay television service beamed off Intelsat K. The channel will comprise segments from four Spanish-language television channels originated in the US, Mexico and South America for the Spanish market.

elite, often work together to get their message to the public. The government still holds the power to distribute broadcasting licenses and to enforce some regulations, like those on content, and continues to distribute government advertising, which is increasingly important in the Venezuelan crisis – the advertising market contracted from about $200 million a year to less than $80 million in the first six months of Caldera's presidency.

The state-owned television network, Venezolana de Televisión, VTV, transmits commercial programming through Channels 8, 11 and 12 and cultural and educational programmes through Channels 5, 6 and 13. Channel 8 is nationwide. Channel 5 barely covers metropolitan Caracas and some parts of the country. The state broadcaster loses money and is deeply and debt. Its outdated studios, production capability and equipment are a pale reflection of Venezuela's politically and economically powerful commercial broadcasting industry – some of which only temporarily happens to be in the hands of the government.

6 *Peru*

This chapter on Peru is the first of three chapters looking at countries with more fragmented broadcasting industries, where domestic broadcasting historically did not develop into a strong monopolistic industry. In each country – Peru, Argentina, and Colombia – this fragmentation was the result of the types of relationships between the state and the broadcasting industry, and the accommodations, or lack of them, the state and the broadcasting industry were able to reach. The fragmentation of the Peruvian broadcasting industry was the result of the weaknesses of the country's civilian regimes, who were unable to build a strong private industry, and of the media's failure to reach an accommodation with the state while it was under the control of the military. The current splintering of the Peruvian broadcasting industry is largely the result of this inability of Peruvian rulers to reach an accord with the media, due to weaknesses within the Peruvian state and political parties.

Major swings in policy between *laissez-faire* and government intervention marked the long relationship between the state and the Peruvian media. The frustrations of social movements to achieve political representation and economic reform and the historical weakness of the Peruvian state were important motives in the military's attempt between 1968 and 1980 to profoundly reform the Peruvian state and society, including the introduction of radically new broadcasting policies. The nationalist broadcasting policies carried out by the Peruvian military were a reaction against the historical inability of Peruvian society to construct a Peruvian state with a national project. The ultimate result of these reforms, however, was government censorship and the strengthening of the private broadcasting industries. Yet, in the years that followed, the Peruvian broadcasting industry, unlike industries in other countries, was unable to maintain its growth, mainly as a result of the chaos and weakness of the Peruvian state (and economy) and its increasing inability to govern the country. Without a relationship with a strong state or political party, Peru was unable to develop a powerful domestic broadcasting industry.

Early Peruvian radio and broadcasting regulations

Many of the problems facing Peruvian broadcasting in 1968 when the military seized control of the country had their origin in the early years of the 20th century.

Between 1919 and 1930 Peru was ruled by Augusto B Leguia. Leguia was fond of publicity and public appearances and at a relatively early date recognised the value of radio for propaganda and public relations. In 1924 Leguia inaugurated the first Peruvian radio station, the state-owned, commercially operated 'Peruvian Broadcasting Company'. The station, however, was not a commercial success and two years later it went bankrupt and was taken over by the British-owned Marconi Company, already the owner of most of the station's equipment. The station continued to broadcast under government control, and the employees became employees of the Peruvian Post Office, also largely owned by Marconi. No other state or private radio station went on the air until 1935.

Leguia's overthrow in 1930 was followed by almost ten years of political chaos, often accompanied by violence and bloodshed. Manuel Prado was elected president in 1939 and governed Peru in a period of relative stability during the Second World War. In 1945, Jose Luis Bustamante y Rivero was elected president. By this time approximately ten private commercial radio stations, now organised in the National Association of Peruvian Broadcasters, ANRAP, had gone on the air (Gargurevich 1987).

Under the General Telecommunications Law enacted in 1947 Bustamante attempted to establish some order in the uncontrolled growth of commercial broadcasting. The law, the first to address communication since a 1916 law regulating the post office, telegraph, and telephone services, established several administrative and technical norms for private broadcasting. The next year Bustamante was ousted by General Manuel Odria, who ruled Peru for the next six years, favouring the traditional agricultural sectors of the economy over national industry. Reversing Bustamante's attempt to regulate commercial broadcasting, Odria allowed private broadcasters to operate commercially largely outside any government regulation.

During Odria's rule the Peruvian Armed Forces established the Centre of Military Studies (Centro de Altos Estudios Militares, CAEM). The military placed their motto – Ideas are to be explained not imposed – over the front gate. CAEM, a centre where intellectuals of the right as well as the left could be found teaching Peruvian military officers, began the task of forming an educated professional armed forces. Partially through the actions of CAEM, groups within the military reached the conclusion that to save the country and their own institution from the revolutionary upsurge of the masses, they had to take the lead in transforming rather than defending the established socio-economic order.

Manuel Prado was elected president for a second time in elections held in 1956. His second term of office witnessed growing revolts in the rural areas, seizures of farmlands, and massacres of landholders. Social pressure mounted in the cities and the mining areas. Students and labour organisations like the National Federation of Bank Employees and the Federation of Peruvian Mine Workers now exercised an important role in politics. One of the first occupations of lands by the revolutionary guerrilla movements occurred near Cuzco, and the army was ordered to repress the rural uprisings, establishing a traumatic and bloody precedent.

The introduction of television

Television was introduced in Peru during Prado's second term. Prado enacted a General Broadcasting Law with technical norms and fiscal requirements for future television licensees. In 1958, with the collaboration of UNESCO, Prado set up an educational and cultural TV station in the Ministry of Education. The Prado law reserved a TV channel for the government and one for the Ministry of Education. A subsequent decree declared television a protected industry and exempted imports of broadcast and studio equipment from tariffs and custom duties.

The first Peruvian television station was a state channel, but private broadcasters did not allow the government to develop its communication resources much further. Two associations of private broadcasters protested what they considered to be the state interference in the free development of the national communications market. Soon after going on the air with its own channel, Prado authorised four private TV licenses. Channel 4 was given to the Compañia Peruana de Radiodifusion Radio America, a private radio chain founded in 1942. A license for Channel 9 was given to the Compañia Peruana de Producciones Radiales y TV, a company set up by the Miro Quesada family, owners of El Comercio, the leading Lima daily. Channel 9 had an agreement with NBC for programming and equipment. Channel 2 went to Radiodifusora Victora, also a radio chain. Finally, Channel 13 (later changed in Channel 5) went to Panamericana Television, of the Panamericana Radio chain, in partnership with Goar Mestre, former owner of Cuban television, and with the US TV network CBS.

The military return

Nationalist candidate Haya de la Torre won the 1962 presidential elections. The military, however, staged a coup before he could take office and, within the next year, among other measures, passed laws for an agrarian reform, a national planning institute, and a national telecommunications council. The military called for elections in 1963, which were won by Fernando Belaunde Terry. The new civilian administration, however, failed to deliver the nationalist reforms the military demanded. Belaunde reneged on his campaign promise to carry out the agrarian reform and to nationalise the foreign-owned petroleum companies.

Belaunde was especially obliging with the private broadcasters, who had grown to be an important force as a result of government chaos and lack of policy. Although Peruvian television reached slightly under 300,000 households, it attracted over half the advertising in the country, while newspapers (25 per cent), radio (15 per cent) and magazines (4 per cent) divided up the rest (Neyra 1974, 56). In 1968, with the support of the right-wing controlled congress, Belaunde passed a new broadcasting law. Article 5 of the Basic Norms of Broadcasting declared the commercial activities of the Peruvian private broadcastings to be in the public interest and lowered the costs of a commercial broadcasting license.

The military's discontent with Belaunde reached its limit in 1968 with a public outcry over his mishandling of the new contract with the International Petroleum Company, owner of most of Peru's petroleum resources. On 3 October 1968, the head of the joint military command, General Juan Velasco Alvarado, backed by a group of colonels, overthrew Belaunde and set up the Revolutionary Government of the Armed Forces (Lowenthal 1975). The Revolutionary Government of the Armed Forces had ample time to prepare their entrance in national politics. The establishment of CAEM in 1952 and the army's extensive training programming produced a nationalist, professional officer corps, many of whom were recruited from the lower economic strata and the rural areas. The traumatic experience of putting down the rural protests and guerilla movements of the mid-1960s had strengthened the military's belief in the importance of a strong state, national planning, and social and economic reforms as guarantees of stability and security. Once in power the military moved quickly and with a great sense of legitimacy to nationalise the Peruvian petroleum deposits and implement policies of state-directed reform and institutional change.

Few of the reforms proposed by the Peruvian military were new to Latin America. It was the first time, however, that a programme of land reform, educational development, and national industrialisation was carried out in Peru, a country of great inequalities of wealth and a rigid social structure. It was also the first time that a government had strengthened the instruments of the state, decreased the power of the landed oligarchies, and regulated foreign investment. When the military took over Peru in 1968, Peru was considerably behind most of its neighbours with regard to various pressing economic and political reforms, and there was considerable consensus on what needed to be done (Lowenthal 1975, 30). In general the military's policies combined public resources with those of private capital in order to enlarge the internal market and integrate the country socially and economically.

Broad cultural reforms in the national education system and the mass media accompanied the military's economic and social policies. The military aimed to encourage the cultural unity of the country, re-vindicate traditional national cultural values, and guarantee the people's support for the military's wider, often controversial, economic and social policies. The military reforms affected land tenure, water rights, labour-management relations, public administration, and the economy in general. Considerable domestic opposition to many of the measures came from those most affected by the reforms. Internationally, the Peruvian military maintained a strong Third World position. They supported the non-aligned movement and joined calls for a new world economic order. The military established diplomatic relations with the socialist countries of Europe and was the first Latin American country to break the US imposed economic and diplomatic boycott of Cuba.

A flurry of new laws, institutions, and reforms marked the first years of the military government. The military's platform was nationalist, corporatist, participatory, and authoritarian. Nationalist sentiment fuelled the expropriations of foreign industries as well as the new-found use for the Quechua language and the symbols of the country's Indian heritage. The corporatist/participatory principles of the regime powered the creation of an organised social sector within each industry and branch of economic activity. The regime's authoritarianism fed its desire to .control public opinion. The three characteristics were interwoven in the military's programmes. Some of the institutions set up by the military in the broadcasting sector, for example, were inspired more by the need to control public opinion than by concerns for national culture or participation. Other measures were the product of participatory principles (Peirano 1978).

The communication sector under the military

Most of the changes in the Peruvian communications sector and especially in television took place during the first years of the regime. In general the changes were directed at freeing the communication sector from its dependence on foreign companies, increasing the role of the state, and placing the mass media at the service of national education and cultural policies. Television policies were followed almost five years later by reforms in the national press, including the expropriation of the Lima newspapers and the plan, announced but never carried out by the military, to turn the newspapers over to 'organised sectors of the community'.

The guiding document of the military's strategy was the 'Inca Plan,' released in 1974 but said to have been prepared earlier. The plan diagnosed the national communication sector as deficient and unable to integrate the national territory. It criticised the mainly foreign-owned telephone companies and the handful of large commercial broadcasting companies for monopolising and distorting public opinion. The plan proposed the modernisation, organisation and integration of the public telecommunications services under state ownership. Broadcasting would be exploited by the state or in association with the private sector and would be transferred gradually to the organised representatives of Peruvian society. According to the plan, (*Plan del Gobierno Revolucionario de la Fuerza Armada*) the communication system, under state control, would induce social and economic development, contribute to national integration, and guarantee national defence (Rocca 1975).

In December 1968 the Peruvian military set up the Ministry of Transportation and Communications, charged with directing, developing, and regulating postal and telecommunication services. In March 1969 the government enacted the General Law of Transportation and Communication, setting up the General Direction of Communications in charge of all national and international communications. Between 1970 and 1973 the military expropriated and nationalised the holdings of IT&T, Ericsson, and other foreign companies in the Peruvian telephone market. Entel-Peru, established in 1969, provided the public services of telecommunications.

In 1971 the military established the National Institute of Educational Television (INTE) to produce educational programmes for television and control the importation of television programming. INTE produced some of the educational programming later shown on Peruvian television like *La Casa del Carton*. The same year the Revolutionary Government enacted a General Law of Telecommunications (Decreto Ley No. 199020). The law replaced previous laws, regulated all aspects of telecommunications including broadcasting, telephones, telegraph, and the postal service, and changed the structure and definition of Peru's telecommunication services. Article 2 gave the state the power to direct, promote, use, regulate, and control telecommunications and placed telecommunications at the service of the community as a tool for social and economic development. It also gave telecommunications employees the right to participate in the profits of their companies (Ortega and Romero 1976).

Citing excessive commercialisation (37 per cent) and foreign content (64 per cent), Article 16 of the law expropriated 51 per cent of the stock of the private television companies (and 25 per cent of the stock of radio companies). In the future, TV channels could only be exploited by state-owned companies or by companies where the state was the majority share holder. No foreign investment was allowed in a TV station, and no single individual could own more than seven radio and television stations or more than one radio and television station in the same department. The law required that the content of television be oriented toward the humanistic, cultural and social formation of the people, charging TV with supporting the national educational reform and other changes necessary for national development. Article 20 required that channels broadcast all government messages of national interest and one hour daily of cultural and educational programming. The channels were given three years to comply with Article 22 requiring that 60 per cent of all programming and all advertising be produced nationally (Mattos 1981).

The General Law of Telecommunications contained none of the participatory measures that would be included in later policies such as the expropriation of the Lima newspapers. Despite the requirements for educational and cultural content, the Government's main interest in television was the control of public opinion. The military became a partner with the private sector in television mainly to guarantee television's favourable political content. The regime imposed few cultural changes on the medium, and the continuation of television as a commercial enterprise financed by advertising left little room for experimentation or subsidised cultural and artistic productions. Although nominally under state political control, Peruvian television was still operating under a commercial broadcasting model

At the time the telecommunications law went into effect, Lima had one state-owned and one cultural TV station and four privately owned commercial stations. There were 13 private commercial stations outside Lima that formed part of the networks of the four Lima channels. All four commercial channels in Lima were partly owned by the US television networks. Within the next two years the military government expropriated the remaining 49 per cent of the stock of the two weakest stations, Channels 2 and 11, and took them off the air. Even in the greatly reduced television market, the remaining channels claimed they were financially unable to comply with the directives regarding national content and educational programming. In January 1972 the Ministry of Education set up the Office of Collective Communication charged with establishing the norms for broadcasting content and advertising. A year later, the government added another institution to the communications sector, INICTEL, the National Institute of Research and Training in Telecommunications. INICTEL was financed with the proceeds of a 2 per cent tax on the earnings of the companies that exploited the public services of broadcasting and telecommunications. Even with these two new institutions, the Peruvian government was unable to enforce the regulations on national content and advertising. Channels 4 and 5 continued to broadcast many of the same imported soap operas and television series that they had used before the military takeover (Ortega and Romero 1976).

SINADI and Telecentro

The absence of national content continued to plague the military's media policies. Between 1967 and 1973, approximately 60 per cent of the content of Peruvian television was imported. In 1974, the regime set up, Telecentro, a state-owned production company, to produce programmes for Channels 4 and 5. Telecentro was yet another new institution in the expanding constellation of organisation in the state-owned communication sector. The next month the military inaugurated SINADI, a national information system charged with coordinating government advertising and the national development plan and insuring that the contents of the mass media satisfied the cultural, educational and entertainment needs of the people. SINADI was also in charge of the state-owned broadcasting company, Enrad Peru, the state-owned telecommunications company Entel Peru, and the educational television institutions of the ministry of education INTE. In this way one institution controlled all aspects of broadcasting infrastructure, transmission, administration and production. Other SINADI organisations included a government information service, a publishing house, and a national film production company (Tello 1986).

Genaro Delgado Parker, the former owner of Channel 5 and the owner of the remaining Panamericana companies, was named head of Telecentro.[1] Foreign content on Peruvian television dipped slightly in the years following the establishment of Telecentro, to 58.97 per cent in 1974, 59.01 per cent in 1975 and 56.59 per cent in 1976. In the following years, however, it climbed steadily to 69.46 per cent in 1979 and 71.84 per cent in 1980.

The executive office of the national information system was the Central Office of information (OCI) in charge of government information, public relations and the press. OCI was also responsible for television censorship. It blocked several initiatives to produce socially innovative programmes like those proposed on a Lima slum reconstruction project and on a meeting of bishops from the Third World held in Lima. OCI routinely closed down, eventually permanently the only independent political programme on Peruvian television, *Quipu* (Gargurevich 1987).

The expropriation of the Lima dailies

Soon after the formation of SINADI, the military's relationship with the press, until then conflictive and often repressive as in the case of the closing down of opposition publications, changed radically. On 26 July, 1974, the government announced the expropriation of all the Lima newspapers with a national circulation and their transfer to the 'organised sector' of Peruvian society – the peasant organisations, the cooperatives, the labour and teachers unions, and professional and cultural groups. The transfer of the Lima dailies to the different social organisations never took place, however, and during the year following their expropriation, the papers were run by military appointed directors (Peirano 1978).

In August 1975, a change in leadership within the military signaled a shift in the direction and intensity of the military's reform programme. The expropriation and 'socialisation' of the Lima papers, probably the most controversial measure of the military in the area of communication, was never completed, although the

---

1 Telecentro was owned equally by the Panamericana Television channel (51 per cent government-owned), the Compania Peruana de Radiodifusión Channel 4 (51 per cent government-owned), and the Panamericana production company (17 per cent government-owned). The majority stock holder was Panamericana with 44 per cent of the stock. The government owned 39.7 per cent and the Companía Peruana de Radiodifusión the remaining 16.3 per cent.

newspapers remained under government control until 1980 when a newly elected civilian government returned them to their original owners. The new leader of the military government, General Morales Bermudez, announced the continuation of the cultural programme and reforms of the previous administration. The plan of the second phase of the military regime was called plan 'Tupac Amaru' and contained an even more radical analysis of the media than the first phase. The Tupac Amaru plan condemned the lack of nationally produced radio and television, programmes, movies, and books. It recommended the total expropriation of the television channels and their transfer to organised sectors of society, the complete state control of Telecentro, the reduction of television transmission time and advertising, limits on imported films and publications, the transfer of radio station to different social organisations, the creation of regional government newspapers, and the expansion of domestic and international government information services (Gargurevich 1987).

The military, however, were in no condition to carry out these or the many others reform measures they proposed. They were increasingly unable to meet the demands of the lower classes or reconcile the interests of labour with the private sector. The military's strategy of national development for national security was falling apart. Peru's growing national debt and crisis in its balance of payments obliged the military to adopt unpopular measures recommended by the International Monetary Fund like the devaluation of the currency, the reduction in public expenditures, increased taxes, and the elimination of most wage and price controls (Tello 1986).

The return to civilian rule

Unable to maintain their hold on the state or manage the economy, in 1978 the military announced elections for a Constitutional Assembly that would prepare a new constitution and pave the way for the return of a civilian government. During the military's last two years in power they authorised the introduction of colour television and gave Channels 4 and 5 licenses to operate commercial TV stations in cities in the interior of the country. The government dissolved Telecentro and no longer enforced the regulations on national content.

In 1980 the newly elected civilian administration of Fernando Belaunde returned the Lima newspapers and the expropriated radio and TV stations to their original owners, in some cases compensating them with tax breaks and reduced tariffs on imported equipment and programming. Peru returned to an almost wholly privately owned and commercially operated broadcasting system. The two remaining national TV networks were hardened to government intervention and operated largely without competition from the smaller channels that had disappeared under military rule. Indirectly, the growth and consolidation of these national networks was one of the legacies of the military's intervention in broadcasting. This consolidation coincided with a large increase in television homes. Coverage of TV had increased during the military's rule from about 18 per cent of the homes in Lima in 1972 to almost 60 per cent of the homes in the capital city in 1980. Television's coverage outside Lima also grew with the introduction of new regional channels.

Broadcasting in Peru into the 21st century

The present broadcasting environment in Peru has become more fragmented than the two networks that emerged in the period immediately following the twelve years of military rule. In part this is the result of the political chaos of the country over the last years in which presidents from three different and antagonistic political parties have held office – Fernando Belaunde, followed by Alan García and Alberto Fujimori. Presently, Peru has close to 246 television stations, many of which are affiliated to a network. Peruvian television receives 54 per cent of all advertising, followed by 21 per cent for radio, and only 18 per cent for the press. Lima has seven VHF channels and one UHF channel. The three oldest VHF channels, 4, 5 and 7, all have national coverage.

Panamericana Television, Channel 5 PANTEL is owned by the Delgado Parker family,[2] the owner of industries, banks, real estate, and Telcable, a Lima cable system. Channel 5 covers the country via PanAmSat.[3] Companía Peruana de Radiodifusión, Channel 4 America TV is now owned by Mexican Televisa. In January 1990 it began national coverage, also on PanAmSat. Radio Television Peruana, Channel 7 RTP-TV is the government-owned channel. It has national coverage on Intelsat and the national microwave network, both services of Entel Peru, the national telecommunications company.

Numerous smaller channels have been set up since 1980. Companía Latinoamericana de Radiodifusión, Channel 2 began operating in 1982 and covers the department of Lima and surrounding areas with strong audience ratings. Compania Andina de Radiodifusión, Channel 9 began operating in 1984 and covers the department of Lima and surrounding areas. R.B.C. Promotores, Channel 11, the only Peruvian channel that is publicly traded on the national stock exchange, has approximately one hundred thousand small stock holders. Thirty per cent of its stock is owned by Ricardo Belmont Cassinelli, a well known television personality who, on the basis of his television fame, was elected mayor of Lima in November 1989.

Channel 11 began operating in 1983 and covers the department of Lima and surrounding areas. Empresa Radiodifusora 1160, Channel 13 began operating in 1986 covers the Department of Lima and surrounding areas. Difusora Universal de Television Channel 27 UHF began operating in 1983 as the first and only attempt at a pay television system with an encoded signal.

Today Peruvian television in general is supportive of the Fujimori regime, a popularly elected president who, in April 1992 closed Parliament and assumed quasi-dictatorial powers to rule the country. In fact, in order to increase their audiences most Peruvian television stations are openly supportive of the president, who, despite his non-democratic actions, enjoys a wide popular following (Gutierrez 1992, 39-41). Following a pattern established earlier in Brazil and Mexico, opposition, if any, to Fujimori, does not come from broadcasting.

The explosion of new television channels and continued political instability in Peru mean it is probably too late for the present authoritarian regime to foster a

---

2   Hector Delgado Parker, an owner of Panamericana, was one of the principal advisors of President Alan Garcia. In November 1989, he was kidnapped, tried and later released by the terrorist groups MRTA (Movimento Revolucionario Tupac Amaru), allegedly for his collaboration with the government.

3   In 1992 controlling interest in PanAmSat was acquired by Mexico's Televisa.

strong national media that could serve its needs. The conditions in Peru, however, are similar today to those that faced Brazil in 1964 at the beginning of the military's long rule in that country. The time is ripe for a strong relationship to form between an increasingly authoritarian state and a monopolistic private commercial broadcasting industry.

7 *Colombia*

Colombia presents a unique case of the fragmentation of a domestic broadcasting industry. In Peru fragmentation was the result of the weaknesses of the political parties and their inability, and that of the military rulers, to work with the broadcasters. In Colombia, however, fragmentation was the outcome of the strength of a political system, more concerned with maintaining the broadcasting system's 'parity' between the two traditional ruling parties than with imposing its social or political goals on radio or television. The power of radio to mobilise popular sentiment and direct political events was clipped in the late 1940s after a popular revolt nearly destroyed the country's political balance. Television, originally set up under a dictatorship mainly for propaganda purposes, later became one of the spoils of the political pact for power sharing among the elites. As a result of this political accommodation, no strong Colombian broadcasting monopoly evolved, despite the commercial interests that flourished within the government-owned television stations.

The historical political and economic fragmentation of the Colombian media appears to be disappearing. This process is fuelled by the recent growth of FM radio, the emergence of different forms of television delivery, including cable and pay-TV, but, more importantly, by the evolution of the Colombian political system and the end of the pact between the two traditional parties. In a turn of events unique in the region to Colombia, the growing political strength of the Colombian media industries, rather than from television, is drawing much of its power from two large private radio networks, owned by domestic industrial conglomerates. At the same time, new legislation on television provides safeguards against monopolistic practices and opens the door to the creation of more private television channels throughout the country.

Early Colombian radio and the breakdown of the old order

Colombian radio made up for its relatively late birth in 1929 by growing rapidly after 1931 when a president from the ruling Liberal Party changed the tax system to make commercial operations of radio stations profitable. Using a formula particular to Colombia and later applied to television, the first radio stations were public-private hybrids. The Colombian government rented time slots on state-owned radio stations to private companies who in turn exploited them commercially by selling advertising time.

Commercial radio stations grew in the 1930s. In 1935, for example, Colombian manufacturers of tobacco products, textiles, beer, foodstuffs, and pharmaceutical companies grouped together to set up a large regional radio station on which they could advertise their products. Many Colombian radio station owners also were distributors of foreign-made radio sets like Telefunken, RCA, and Philips. Radio soon became a popular medium throughout the country. When Argentine tango idol Carlos Gardel was killed in an air crash in Medellin, Colombia in 1935, the news of this death was broadcast direct on radio from the scene of the crash at Las Playas airport in one of the first live radio news programmes in Latin America. The 17 Colombian stations registered in 1934 jumped to 44 stations by 1939, and, two years later, to 70 (Pareja 1984).

On 9 April, 1948, Jorge Eliecer Gaitan, the popular leader of the Liberal Party and candidate for the presidency of Colombia, was gunned down on the streets of Bogota. In the mass riots that followed, numerous radio stations throughout the country, including state-owned stations, were taken over by Gaitan's sympathisers who attempted to channel popular outrage and resentment against the Conservative government into a revolutionary movement. They almost succeeded, and the country was on the verge of civil war between followers of the Liberal and Conservative parties. When government forces regained control of the country, they imposed a state of siege, revoking all existing radio licenses and altering the existing radio regulations to bring radio firmly under government control and restrict all news and political content. Although Colombian radio continued to expand commercially after 1948, and the major radio networks established strong ties with domestic industry, advertising agencies and powerful political groups, as a result of the government controls, radio never again played a significant role in Colombian politics (Tellez 1974).

Following the assassination of Gaitan and the popular outrage it inflamed, Colombia was placed under authoritarian rule, culminating in the military regime of General Rojas Pinilla between 1953 and 1957. In 1958 Colombia's traditional Liberal and Conservative parties removed Rojas. The two parties then signed a pact called the 'National Front' in which they agreed to alternate the presidency and share government posts for the next sixteen years. The party leaders saw the agreement as an immediate alternative to the military regime and a long-term solution to the civil wars and social violence that had ravaged Colombia for the better part of the century.

The National Front created the conditions for economic growth and social development. At the same time, it fostered a system of personal political patronage that blocked the access to power and participation in government of other parties and social groups. The reduced scope of political activities allowed under the agreement – during 15 of the 20 years between 1958 and 1978 Colombia was ruled under a state of siege – and the inability of third party initiatives to gain access to power, left significant social sectors outside the Colombian political system. Few participated in elections and support for revolutionary guerrilla movements grew. The Colombian broadcasting industries matured within the context of political accommodation between the two traditional ruling parties and the exclusion from power of third parties and all other popular movements.

The introduction of television

Colombian television began in 1954, one year after General Rojas Pinilla came to power. Rojas, initially brought to office by the traditional parties to restore domestic order, was looking for ways to create his own base of popular support. Rojas had placed the Colombian newspapers, largely controlled by the traditional parties, under strict state control. Censorship alone, however, was not sufficient. Rojas felt he needed his own form of communication with the people. Coffee prices, the source of 85 per cent of Colombia's export earnings, were high, and the dictator, taking advantage of the economic bonanza, much of which flowed into the state coffers, imported television transmission and studio equipment and set up a government television channel under the Office of Information and the Press of the Presidency.

Soon after Colombia's first, and for many years only, television channel went on the air, coffee prices dropped on the world market. Decree 3418, implemented under Rojas Pinilla in 1954, defined television as a public service, financed from the national budget. Two years later the government felt it could no longer afford to finance television solely as a public service. It issued Decree 2427, limiting the provision of television services to the state but permitting the commercial sponsorship of television programmes by private companies (Fox 1973). Despite the change in regulation, commercial sponsorship of Colombian television did not begin on a mass scale until after Rojas' ouster. Private firms were hesitant to have their names linked through government-controlled television to an increasingly unpopular dictatorship. At the same time, Rojas was reluctant to grant too much power on his government television system to the private firms that increasingly were supporting his political opponents.

The fragmentation of television

Following Rojas' removal in 1957 the state television channel remained under the office of the presidency. In 1960, the government television channel was transferred to the Division of Radio and Television of the Ministry of Communication. Three years later the government set up Inravisión, a 'decentralised' public institute under the executive branch of government, to run Colombian television. Inravisión, a public-private hybrid, managed Colombian television for the next twenty-two years. It was a state-owned, commercially operated television system. The infrastructure and social services of television were state-run and financed. The private sector provided commercial entertainment, and advertising through companies called programmers, and the two ruling parties jointly managed television's power to inform and shape opinions through the control of news programmes. It was an accommodation in which no one actor – the rival political parties, the media owners, or advertisers – could gain ascendancy (Martinez 1978).

Inravisión separated the Colombian government from the direct sale of advertising. This became the function of the private programmers' which acted as intermediaries between Inravisión and advertisers. Inravisión was in charge of transmitting TV signals and renting its production facilities and airtime to programmers. The programmers produced or purchased a television programme to fill the airtime they rented from Inravisión and sold time on the programme to advertisers. The Colombian president named Inravisión's board of directors. This gave the executive tight control of Inravisión's budget, programming schedule, and airtime. The board was composed of the director of Inravisión, the Ministers of Communication and Education, and two representatives of the president. After the initial costs of equipment and infrastructure, and new major capital investments like satellite ground stations, Inravisión's daily operation were financed by the tariffs it charged the programmers for the use of its services and airtime.

Until 1965 Inravisión broadcast only one channel nationwide. That year the government set up a second channel serving the Colombian capital, Bogotá, and surrounding areas. In 1966 the president set up an educational television programme in the Ministry of Education and a programme of adult education for grassroots integration and rural development directed at lower-income audiences (Fondo de Capacitación Popular). Until 1970 Inravisión transmitted the classroom and adult education programmes over its two state-owned, commercially operated channels. In 1970 the government set up a third, publicly financed channel dedicated exclusively to educational and cultural programming (Tellez 1975).

The programmers

The first TV programmer, Caracol Televisora Comercial TVC, was set up in 1955 by two of the largest Colombian radio chains: Caracol and Radio Cadena Nacional RCN. Later, two former-directors of Inravisión: Fernando Gomez Agudelo, the director of television under General Rojas, and Alberto Peñalranda, Gomez's successor in Inravisión, set up their own programmers, Radio Television Internacional RTI and Punch, respectively. The programmers' contacts with Inravision generally ran between one and three years and specified the type of content – children's programmes, domestic soap operas, filmed series – for the specific time slot to be filled.

Although Inravisión set the tariffs it charged the programmers for airtime, it had no control over the prices the programmers charged to advertisers. The rapid increase in the number of programmers indicates that television, even under the restricted form of licensing, was a good business.[1] Despite the large number of programmers, the three original and largest companies – Caracol, Punch and RTI, usually were awarded over half the available hours. Later, the same three companies were awarded over 90 per cent of the time of the second television channel (Fox 1973).

The second channel

By 1965 Inravisión's first channel had achieved national coverage, and the government opened a second regional channel serving Bogotá and its surrounding areas. This time the entire channel was licensed to one programmer, although the state maintained ownership of the license. The channel was rented for five years to

---

1 In 1968, 17 programmers bid for two-year contracts for the 96 hours of airtime available weekly. In 1970 there were 24 programmers, and by 1972 there were 42. The hours available for commercial use also grew. Inravisión issued bids for 112 hours in 1971 and for 134 hours in 1974.

Consuelo de Montejo, who had set up an advertising agency and production company to run the channel in association with ABC World Vision.

ABC's investment in the second channel was one of the rare instances of foreign investment in Colombian television. For the most part the US networks and other possible investors like Time-Life, which by that time had invested in the television industries of most other Latin American countries, did not enter the Colombian market. The sentiment among the US networks was that Colombian broadcasting was highly controlled and restrictive and commercial television's relationship with the state was too uncertain and undefined.[2]

Furthermore, the Colombian advertising market was divided among three large cities – not the case in most other Latin American countries where the market was concentrated in one or, in the case of Brazil, two large metropolitan areas. This geographic fragmentation increased the reluctance of foreign investors to enter the Colombian broadcasting market.

During the five years of its contract, Teletigre, as the second channel was called, with a schedule of about 75 per cent imported programming, surpassed the national channel in the Bogotá area in audiences and advertising. After five years Teletigre's contract was not renewed. Inravisión argued that the channel had competed unfairly because of foreign investment and its ability to sell advertising in blocs of time. (De Montejo was also beginning to acquire a significant political powerbase in the Conservative Party through her television channel.) In the future, Inravisión rented the second channel by individual time slots to many different programmers, returning to the fragmented control of television and ending one of the few potential threats of a powerful domestic media industry.

Although legally separate, the three largest commercial programmers on Colombian television worked together, earning the name 'The Pool'. Each of the three submitted a separate bid to Inravision. The advertising earnings from the three companies were combined and divided equally. The Pool centralised its purchasing of foreign programming and its domestic production capacity. The schedules of the programmes were coordinated to complement each other and benefit the ratings of all three companies, attracting different audiences rather than splitting the same public by, for example, showing two soap operas at the same time on both channels (Fox 1973).

The government exercised little control over the entertainment programming that went out on the airtime it rented to the private programmers. The Liberal and the Conservative Presidents who alternated in office were happy to allow this hybrid pubic-private model of commercial television to develop as long as it did not present a political challenge. The Government did, however, exercise control over news and opinion shows. News programmes were not bid but assigned directly by the president to guarantee the mandatory political parity between the two parties. In the early 1970s new regulations required that all live news programming be filmed before broadcast and given to Inravisión, which often took controversial opinion shows off the air.

The system seemed to work. The state (under first one party and then the other) controlled the political content of television, guaranteeing the two ruling

2 Based on the author's interviews with ABC executives in 1971.

parties equal access to news and opinion shows. The larger programmers became efficient, diversified cultural industries, yet, because of the fragmented nature of Colombian television, never grew big enough to challenge the state.[3] The government was able to balance commercial programming with development and educational programming, transmitted on its cultural and educational broadcasting services. Thus, despite the highly commercial, imported, and oddly monotonous content of Colombian television, for the most part the government was able to avoid charges of misuse of a public service and calls for new national policies.

The delicate equilibrium within the state and between the state and the private sector did not mean that Colombian television stood still. During the 1970s, as in most Latin American countries, the number of broadcasting hours and the size of TV audiences and advertising practically doubled. Between 1970 and 1980, transmission time available for commercial broadcasting increased from 96 to 152 hours weekly; the number of programmers jumped from 17 to 57; and the geographic coverage of television expanded greatly as did the number of people employed by the sector. Between 1974 and 1980 advertising in Colombian television increased tenfold and by 1980 accounted for over half total advertising. Nor did Colombian television lag behind other Latin American countries in the introduction of new audiovisual technologies. During the 1970s Colombian television entered the era of modern telecommunications with the introduction of satellite services and colour transmission.

The Colombian hybrid

The Colombian hybrid system offered advantages to all the parties involved and created few of the tensions present in the broadcasting systems of other Latin American countries. The existence of many small programmers instead of one or two large private channels – as was the case of almost all the other countries – fragmented the economic and political power of the private sector and made it easier for the state to exercise control over news and public opinion. Likewise, the pact between the two traditional parties for the control of the state kept any single party from gaining ascendancy over national television and challenging the private sector, or the other party, through control of television.

The low profile of Colombian television made it less susceptible to public criticism. It was hard to drum up popular or political support for the expropriation of a company that every few years publicly bid for time on a state-owned channel. There was nothing to expropriate. Programmers were essentially intermediaries. This explains the lack of support for television reform in Colombia, or for issues like the New World Information Order, which was not the case in other Latin American countries, notably Peru, Chile and Mexico.

Another factor making Colombian television less controversial was the absence of direct foreign investment. In other Latin American countries foreign investment was often among the most polemic and, for a nationalist state, easiest to attack characteristics of the private television industries. This was not the case of Colombian television. The fractured private sector and the strong state role made

---

3 The exception to this was Teletigre during its five-year contract with Consuelo de Montejo.

Colombian television a high risk for the US television networks. Colombian television, despite its highly commercial content, offered fairly strong cultural and educational services. Educational television services in Colombia in the 1970s were considerable compared to television systems of other Latin American countries. The fractured private sector, the two–party political balance within the government, the absence of contentious foreign investment, and the presence of educational services all decreased the likelihood of a movement for new 'distributive' or nationalist communication policies in Colombia.

The presence of significant guerrilla movements increased in Colombia in the 1970s, and, attempting to capture popular discontent, dissident movements emerged within the two traditional political parties. The basic political structure of the country, however, changed little. In 1977 an attempt was made to introduce some changes in broadcasting. This attempt came at the end of the National Front, the pact between the two traditional parties. It is an indication of the beginning of a new stage in the relationship between the state and the different actors in Colombian television.

A non-policy

In 1977 the first president elected after the National Front,[4] Alfonso Lopez Michelsen (1974-1978) from the Liberal Party, directed his Minister of Communications, a Conservative, to introduce a new television law. If enacted, the law would significantly alter the prevailing distribution of power and resources in Colombian television. The Conservative Party, faced with the prospect of its first real presidential defeat under free elections, feared the return of the Liberal Party as the predominant party in national politics.[5] The Conservatives especially feared the control of television by an incumbent Liberal president. The Conservatives suspected that the Liberals, firmly installed in power without the limitations of the National Front, would use Colombia's centrist system and strong presidential powers to their full advantage.[6] The presidential control of television by a Liberal would leave the Conservatives without access to or participation in what was fast becoming the most important political medium in the country.

In 1976 President Lopez awarded the new bids for television time and distributed the news and opinion programmes. His distribution of news programmes demonstrated the president's great personal power over television programming and news. Lopez gave a news show to his son and, in 1977, set up a government news programme and production company.[7] When the Conservatives found the Liberal Party candidates had an advantage in the TV news programmes of Colombian television, they demanded new television policies, accusing the Liberals of taking unfair advantage of presidential power over Colombian television. The

---

4 An agreement between the two parties to exercise parity in the public sector, however, was still in effect.

5 The Liberal Party ruled the country during much of the previous century and between 1930 and 1945.

6 During the Liberal administration of Carlos Lleras Restrepo (1966-1970), the distribution of news and opinion programmes had favoured the Liberal party. The reverse had occurred during the Conservative administration of Misael Pastrana that followed (1970-1974). At the end of Pastrana's mandate a more balanced distribution had been struck with two national news programmes assigned to each party.

7 President Lopez's family were the largest shareholders of Caracol, one of the three largest TV programmers.

Conservative party proposed that the state relinquish control of TV and turn it over to the private sector. The incumbent Liberals, on the other hand, not only had full access to the government news programme but an advantage over the Conservatives in the distribution of news programmes. In response to the Conservative Party's complaints against his management of television, Lopez offered to make available new TV channels. He proposed continuing state administration for the national channels, but allowing private channels, which could broadcast in colour, to operate locally.[8]

The proposed new local channels would pay a license fee of 5 pesos (about 5 cents) for each inhabitant in the zone reached by the channel. The proposal contained stringent ownership limitations for the local channels – local channels could not form a network or set up relay stations, and the same person could own only one local channel in the same area and only three channels in the entire country. The programmers on the national channels could not receive licenses for the local channels. The proposed legislation did not the change programming or the distribution of news on the national channels. The government justified creating local channels with the argument that the national channels, centralised in Bogotá, limited local access and participation in television. Local channels would open new markets, create jobs, and allow programming content more appropriate to regional needs and cultures. The Liberals argued that private ownership of the local channels would insure freedom of expression, improve the content of Colombian television, and guarantee its economic efficiency and political independence.

Congress did not approve the government's proposed legislation. The local channels, congress observed, could not afford to produce their own material and would use cheaper imported programming. Other critics questioned the advisability of a poor country like Colombia multiplying existing television channels and increasing the people's exposure to advertising. Sectors of the Conservative Party, however, who had supported the proposal, considered the private local channels an answer to their demands for more impartial management and increased access to television, especially as the 1978 presidential elections approached. Likewise, regional politicians supported the unsuccessful bid for new channels.

Later broadcasting policies

In 1985, within a wider political reform movement carried out under Conservative President Belisario Betancur, Inravisión, was moved out from directly under the executive power. It became a slightly more representative public institution with the participation of different social organisations on its board of directors. At about the same time, the Betancur government authorised several small regional TV channels – first TeleAntioquia and, later, TeleCaribe, Telecafé and Telepacifico. These channels followed much the same public-private mix that already existed in the national channels.

By the mid-1980s, the number of private programming companies in government television had dropped to around 28. The four largest programmers (Caracol, RCN, Punch, and RTI) continued to control much of the time on Colombian

8 Inravisión had not authorised colour transmission on the national channels.

television, and smaller programmers, including political parties, grassroots, artistic, and religious organisations received only a couple of hours of airtime a week. The larger programmers had their own studio facilities and produced much of their programmes.[9] These domestic productions were more popular with the Colombian audience than imported series. In 1988, RCN produced 70 per cent of its own programming and RTI 65 per cent. Caracol ran nine hours of national and four and a half hours of imported programming a week. Although the programmers continued to complain of government interference in programme selection and the uncertainty of the bidding system, they all made profits, and their productions were beginning to enjoy export success in foreign markets in the region.

Privatisation and liberalisation

The development of radio and television broadcasting in Colombia in the 1990s demonstrates a continuation with the trends that began to emerge in the 1980s. Within the context of the increasing internationalisation and privatisation of the Colombian economy and a new political balance under the National Constitution of 1991, broadcasting has assumed the following characteristics:

(1) The centralisation of media ownership in a few large multimedia conglomerates;

(2) The ownership of media conglomerates by large industrial groups with the corresponding decrease of influence in the media of traditional 'political' groups;

(3) The growth of regional television channels and of community-owned radio and television stations.

The growing influence of large industrial groups in the Colombian media has resulted in the use of the media to further the political and economic influence of these groups. The new-found power of the private industrial sector in the media was evidenced in confrontations between the Ministries of Finance and of Agriculture and the domestic beer industry over the payment of taxes and other issues. The brewer's radio and TV stations and magazines (Caracol Radio, Caracol Television, *Cromos*, TV Cable) savagely attacked the government and successfully defended their interests. The formation of multimedia also is occurring in the smaller cities among provincial newspapers, cable systems, and TV channels.

In the 1991 bids for TV time, about thirty private 'programmers,' dominated by two large companies, were awarded airtime on the two national channels. The two largest programmers, Caracol and Radio Cadena National (RCN), are parts of the Santodomingo and Ardila Lulle industrial complexes, respectively. Other programmers include independent programmers RTI and Jorge Barón, programmers tied to sectors of political parties (ex-President Pastrana and ex-President López), and journalists (CMI, TV-13). Pay-TV companies, with smaller more elite audiences segments, now operate in Bogotá, Medellín, and Ibagué. The largest pay-TV service, TV Cable in Bogotá, is owned by RCN/Datos y Mensajes and

---

9 Inravisión reduced the 'rent' charged programmers for airtime time for nationally produced and educational programming.

Gramacol (Caracol, RTI, *El Tiempo*). It has seven channels, transmitting 24 hours a day.[10]

Satellite antennas have proliferated, sometimes connected to smaller cable systems, and often pirating the signal from international satellite channels. These smaller community cable companies, operating in both urban and rural areas, often leave a channel free for community access, in addition to the regular fare of the national channels and satellite-delivered services.[11]

Radio networks

The large Colombian radio networks consist of local radio stations, linked nationally through relays. Operating this way, the networks maintain local flavour and the power of a national chain. The two largest networks, RCN and Caracol, together cover 98 per cent of the national territory and about 90 per cent of audiences nationwide. RCN has 58 frequencies registered in the Ministry of Communications and is affiliated with Cadena Basica with 24 more stations, Antena 2 with 22 stations, Rumba Stereo with 21 stations, and Bolero Stereo with 7 stations, for a total of 133 stations. The RCN network includes 34 ground relay stations, a satellite channels, a news and electronic library system, and Radio Internacional de RCN, a station in New York. Caracol has 32 registered frequencies, and controls 147 stations, including those of the recently acquired Radio Sutatenza and a new children's radio station, Colorin Colorado. Since 1992, Caracol has used a channel on PanAmSat to reach the outlying areas of the country. Caracol is expanding its international operations to Panama, Ecuador with Radio Centro, and Miami with Radio Klaridad. The two largest Colombian radio networks have expanded internationally and now own and affiliate radio stations in the United States and Europe and operate their own foreign news operations.

New broadcasting regulations

Under Law 14 of 1991, Inravisión was governed by a National Television Council composed of nine members: The Minister of Communications, a representative of the President, the Minister of Education, the Director of the Colombian Institute of Family Welfare, the Director of the Colombian Institute of Culture, and representatives of the Colombian journalists, the communication schools, The National Academy for Television Action,[12] and the National Academy of Colombian History and Language. Law 14 set the conditions for the bidding process and for the contracts between Inravisión and private companies for the commercial use of the two

---

10 Four of the channels are direct transmissions of ESPN, TNT, HBO Ole and the Cartoon Network. The other three channels are programmed by TV Cable. One of these channels is devoted exclusively to news with newscasts from CNN, CBS and ABC, Univision, Telemundo, ECO and two newscasts from Spain (Telediario and Telediario Internacional). The second channel transmits series, movies and a variety of entertainment programming in English. The third channel, the family channel, transmits foreign and domestic soap operas, series, documentaries, talk shows, and sports in Spanish.

11 This is the case of TeleJericó, transmitting a locally produced news programme and an educational programme prepared by the local school teachers every Friday afternoon.

12 The National Academy for Television Action is a body representing many different community organisations including labour unions, peasants unions, artists, consumers, universities, the Church, the medical professions, and advertising.

national television channels. The contracts ran for six years and were renewable. The conditions for renewal were the fulfilment of the contract for content and performance. To increase competition among the different private companies on the national channels, companies had to operate on one channel or the other, not on both. The new contracts made an effort to separate administratively those companies that were purely entertainment or educational and the more 'political' companies that put on news programmes. The third channel, with more limited geographical coverage, is not contracted out to private companies but programmed directly by Inravisión. Its content was educational and cultural, with programmes forming part of the national basic education system and general cultural programming.

The 1991 Television Law defined the regional television channels as industrial and commercial entities, affiliated with the Minister of Communications through the association of Inravision with regional entities. The regional channels can contract out programming, produce their own, or work through a regional/local partner. The regional channels were governed by a Regional Television Council and a Regional Commission for Television Action.

The 1991 legislation, although containing significant changes in the organisation of Colombian television, did not remain on the books for long. The government had announced intentions to privatise Colombian airwaves, and a new law doing just this was passed in early 1995 under the Presidency of Ernesto Samper. Although the two national channels would not be privatised by 1998 when the contracts with the programmers were up, private television would now be the case for the regional and local channels. The 1995 law, however, maintained some of the public service functions of Colombian broadcasting. Two channels – Channel 3 the cultural channel and a new educational Channel 4 – would remain under state control. All other channels would be privatised, and new local regional channels could be opened immediately. The entire broadcasting operation, including the state-operated channels, would be placed under an independent regulatory commission. Other measures in the new law put limits on some monopolistic practices and on the concentration of media ownership.

The power of multimedia

Historically, the elite-enforced fragmentation of the power of the Colombian media reduced the power of the Colombian media to challenge the state. This pact between the elites was the determinant factor in the evolution of domestic broadcasting. The singularity of the Colombian case, however, is rapidly changing as a result of the end of the elites' political pact, the growing multimedia groups, and their influence on public opinion, especially through radio chains. The Santodomingo group, owner of CARACOL radio and the Ardila Lulle group, owner of RCN radio, both are large TV programmers. In addition to radio and TV, these groups own or control magazines (*Cromos*) and, through their banking enterprises, exercise control over newspapers (*El Espectador*). The daily *El Tiempo* is another example of the formation of multimedia groups. It has purchased newspapers and publishing houses throughout the country, as well as the cable company TV Cable.

The end of the traditional political balance/stalemate between the Liberal and Conservative Parties in Colombia and the absence of a strong third party or popular political movement adds to the growing independent political power of the multimedia. For the first time there is no political interest in the country sufficiently united or powerful to maintain the media fragmented. Colombia appears to be heading belatedly in the same direction as Venezuela – toward a powerful, autonomous domestic media industry with one or two large players. These strong players could act either as watchdog or kingmaker in the new Colombian political configuration.

8 *Argentina*

Argentina demonstrates parallels with Colombia in terms of the politically generated fragmentation of its domestic broadcasting industry and the late development of powerful media monopolies. In the case of Argentina, the fragmentation of domestic broadcasting was first the result of the authoritarian measures of a populist president, Juan Perón, and, later, of the direct control of the media by a succession of military dictatorships. Neither Perón nor the military were able to forge a relationship with a compliant private commercial broadcasting industry. Both resorted to expropriations and government takeovers of radio and television stations. Unlike authoritarian regimes in Mexico and Brazil, the Argentine rulers were unable to sustain viable independent domestic media that were at the same time supportive of their regimes and commercially successful.

With the return to democracy, the emerging multimedia monopolies are beginning to change the face of Argentina broadcasting and politics. The relative political stability of the last two democratically elected regimes, the continued weaknesses of the Argentine political parties, and the liberalisation and deregulation of the Argentine media market have opened the way for the growth of large, politically powerful domestic media industries. For the first time, Argentina is having to address the issues of the impact of media concentration on the consolidation of its democratic institutions.

The growth of Argentine commercial radio

Argentine radio developed swiftly after 1920 when amateur radio buffs transmitted Richard Wagner's opera *Parsifal* from the roof of the Coliseo Theatre in Buenos Aires to about 20 radio sets in existence in the capital city. Their station became the country's first radio station, Radio Argentina. During the early years of radio, Radio Argentina broadcast cultural events from theatres and music halls to a small elite urban audience. A much larger station, Radio Sud América, owned by foreign companies selling radio receivers, went on the air in 1922, and, in 1923, another commercial radio station, Radio Cultura, appeared. The government issues commercial radio licenses for one year at a time. There were no attempts to set up state-owned stations until 1927, however, when the city of Buenos Aires established a municipal cultural radio station.

Between 1916 and 1930, a succession of civilian governments ruled Argentina, representing by and large the fast-growing Argentine middle class. A military coup in 1930 by General Félix Uriburu put an end to this relatively stable period of commercial expansion, inaugurating the 'Década Infame', during which elections continued, although under generally fraudulent conditions. Political censorship of radio was introduced in the country, manifest in the restrictive broadcasting regulations of 1934 (Ulanovsky 1992). In 1937, the Argentine Government set up the National Radio Network.

Despite government censorship, commercial radio networks began to form in the early 1930s, and, by 1940 the Argentine commercial radio stations were organised in three powerful privately owned national networks: Radio El Mundo, Radio Belgrano, and Radio Splendid. The Argentine media, including radio, films, magazines and newspapers, were strongly nationalist and had little of the foreign content and investment that marked the media in many other Latin American countries. The Argentine media could afford to be so; nationalism and the size of the Argentine market – large enough to support the domestic media – kept outsiders away. Later, the pro-Axis stand of Argentina during most of the Second World War curbed US investment in broadcasting and slowed the flow of Hollywood films and US music to the country.

The populist government of President Juan Perón from the mid-1940s to the mid-1950s set much of the future course of the Argentine media. Perón protected domestic media production, defended Argentine national culture, and supported the labour unions of media workers. He also censored films, radio, plays, books, magazines, and television. After an initial period of harassment and censorship, 'on the pretext of promoting national defence and the spiritual needs of the country', (Page 1983, 210) Perón nationalised Argentina's three private radio networks by forcing their owners to sell their stations to the government at reduced prices. (In one case, Perón then returned a network to the management of its original owners under close government supervision.) Perón also placed much of the Argentine press in the hands of his supporters. In 1951, after a long and bitter struggle with director Alberto Gainza Paz, Perón expropriated *La Prensa*, one of the few remaining independent newspapers (Page, 1983).

During the ten years of Juan Perón's rule between 1945 and 1955, the Peronists achieved an almost total monopoly of newspapers by forcing their owners to sell their companies to supporters of Perón. Likewise, radio owners were obliged to sell their stations to the state to be run commercially by individuals close to the president. Perón's close control of the media, either directly or under his cronies, insured the fragmentation of the domestic media industries and reduced their ability to threaten his government. It also guaranteed that the media, under his control, supported his political and economic programmes.

Introduction of television

Perón introduced television in Argentina in 1951. The year before he had sent Jaime Yankelevich, a close supporter and former owner of Radio Belgrano, to the United States to purchase equipment for Channel 7. There were 7,000 television sets in Argentina in 1951; two years later there were 40,000. Between 1951 and the fall of Perón in 1955, only one Argentine television channel, operated by the government, went on the air (Noguer 1985).

The military overthrew Perón in 1955. The new rulers ended the government's monopoly of radio and television and threw the Peronists out of broadcasting. For the next 18 years any person who had held a position in Perón's administration or who claimed allegiance to Perón could not appear in any media in any capacity – as producer, technician, writer, or actor. The military returned newspapers to their former owners but kept most radio stations. Three years after seizing power and three days before turning it over to an elected civilian government, the military introduced commercial television. If the military were not to remain in power, they considered it better to set up some competition to the state-run television, especially if the military were in a position to award licenses to their supporters. They awarded private commercial TV licenses to operate Channel 9, Channel 11, and Channel 13 in Buenos Aires; Channel 7 in Mendoza; and Channel 8 in Mar del Plata. By the time the new private channels went on the air in 1960, 850,000 television receivers were in use in Argentina.

The Argentine law drafted under the military prohibited foreign ownership of television channels; foreign capital entered the TV industry by forming production companies in association with the private channels. From the start, Goar Mestre, owner of television channels in Cuba before the revolution, along with CBS and Time-Life co-owned PROARTEL, the production company associated with Channel 13.[1] Channel 11 of Buenos Aires had a similar association in its production company with ABC. Channel 9 set up a production company with NBC. Argentine law also prohibited television networks. The three Buenos Aires channels skirted this prohibition by affiliating the stations in the interior of the country with their production companies. In 1970 PROARTEL, a production company rather than a TV channel, had 17 affiliates.

In order to attract foreign investment, the military and civilian governments that followed Perón authorised the free transfer of earnings and capital of foreign companies operating in Argentina. Between 1958 and 1959 foreign investment in the country jumped from about eight million dollars to over 200 million. Foreign investors and advertisers changed the face of the Argentine media. Television series, magazines, and comic books imported from the United States and Mexico replaced Argentina productions, further fuelling the exodus of Argentine artists and writers triggered by the military's media ban on Perón's followers. The military ruled Argentina for almost two decades more, with two short, unsuccessful attempts at civilian governments.

The return of Perón

In 1973 Perón was re-elected President of Argentina, leading him to observe sardonically that when the Peronists had all the media they were thrown out, and when they had none at all, they won the elections.[2] His administration coincided with the expiration of the 15-year television licenses that had been awarded by the

---

1   In addition to PROARTEL, Mestre had investments in Peruvian and Venezuelan commercial television.

2   Cited by Oscar Landi 1992.

military in 1958. Instead of awarding new TV licenses, or renewing the existing licenses, Perón nationalised Argentine television, declaring it in the public interest (Muraro 1988, 116). He also expropriated the equipment, buildings and furniture of the private production companies and placed new directors in the 'nationalised' TV channels. Television content and commercial operations, however, continued much the same as under private ownership. For three years, until a military coup overthrew the Peronist administration in 1976, the three government-owned channels broadcast in the midst of economic chaos, political uncertainty, and rampant corruption.

Perón's second presidency worked under the principle that the mass media, especially broadcasting, should be controlled by the state. Perón pushed through Congress a series of changes in the ownership, control, financing, and legal structure of the media. Most of these measure were in the direction of increased political control. A new tax on advertising decreased the earnings of the private media and increased state control. Another measure banned the use of international wire services by the national media (Muraro 1988).

The media under the military

In 1976 the Argentine military seized control of the country from Perón's widow and vice president. The military swiftly enacted a series of measures that were of immediate benefit to the private media. The military junta removed the tax on advertising and greatly increased government advertising in the private media – by 60 per cent in the first year. However, as in Brazil, Chile, and Uruguay, at the same time they increased advertising, the military imposed a regime of terror on the independent media (Muraro 1988).

The media were obliged to adhere to the National Security Doctrine of the Argentine military. The Junta established unlimited jail terms for directors of newspapers, radio and television stations who published or broadcast information on the guerrilla groups operating in the country. Ten-year jail terms were set for anyone who published or broadcast information criticising the armed forces, including any mention of the gross violations of human rights carried out daily by the military.

The military junta that seized power in 1976 murdered journalists, closed newspapers, censored publications, blacklisted journalists and artists, and banned foreign and Argentine films, books and magazines. The military expropriated *La Opinion* and jailed and tortured its owner Jacobo Timmerman. Soldiers frequently seized and burned entire editions of local magazines and threatened and kidnapped labour leaders from the media industries. With rare exceptions like the English-language *Buenos Aires Herald*, few newspapers dared give space or time to the leaders of the disbanded political parties, and even fewer ran the paid announcements of the Argentine human rights groups (Landi 1988). The Mothers of the Plaza de Mayo, mutely walking around the square in front of the Presidential palace, with their white kerchiefs embroidered with the names of their lost children, were a direct result of the ravages of repression. Deprived of any access to the mass media, the mothers invented a new form of communication with new symbols to denounce the military's kidnappings of their children and grandchildren.

Despite the Argentine military's declared allegiance to a free market economy, the military maintained tight control over the Buenos Aires television channels, nationalised by Perón in the early 1970s. The military developed a corrupt and complex system of re-sales with advertisers and their clients and paid for lavish TV advertising campaigns to defend their economic and social policies and attack their enemies. While censorship severely limited the Argentine media during the military regime, the impact of the regime's economic polices on consumer spending had an even worse effect on some media. Newspaper and magazine circulation dropped by almost half, and domestic book publishing and film production registered similar falls (Muraro 1988).

The return of democracy

Following the Argentine military's defeat in the Falkland/Malvinas Islands, elections were held and Raúl Alfonsín was elected president. One major challenge facing the civilian rulers who won the elections in 1983 was to establish democratic media policies. Perón's previous goals of cultural nationalism had lost their force in a country faced with crushing economic problems and fed up with dictatorship. New goals reflected a concern for pluralism and for protection from state interference for media and audiences alike. President Alfonsín found his government the legal owner of media it was unable to understand or regulate because of their size, complexities, and layers of corruption. The new democracy removed censorship and transferred one state-owned TV channel to the private sector. Private broadcasters linked to the state-owned channels, however, having grown strong under the military, mounted a campaign against any further government-supported changes in the media. Their campaign was based on a fear that new media owners could be linked to the president's party or simply introduce a new element of competition in an already weak system. For owners of existing media, the relatively weak state-run TV stations were preferable to strong new private stations. Working against these limitations, despite numerous attempts, little was accomplished in domestic media policy during the Alfonsín administration (Landi 1988). Between 1984 and 1989 only two television licenses were transferred from the state to private industry. Channel 9 was transferred to Alejandro Romay. Channel 2 of La Plata was awarded to Hector Ricardo García, the owner of the newspaper *Crónica*, the radio station Colonia (transmitting to Buenos Aires from Uruguay), and the magazines *Flash* and *Esto*.[3]

The 1989 presidential elections were the first elections held in Argentina in sixty years in which a transition took place from one civilian president to another. This first open competition among political parties was marked with extensive use of modern campaign techniques, including public opinion polls, audience research, and the exploitation of mass media, in which television played a central role (Landi 1992). An analyst of the 1989 presidential campaign (Enrique Zuleta-Puceiro, 1992), points out that the use of television, although massive, planned, and technically sophisticated, was always to support, replicate, and consolidate styles and discourse defined in earlier campaign settings more familiar to the candidates. This meant grandiose public ceremonies and press coverage for the Union Civico Radical and marches around the perimeters of large cities for the Peronists (Carlos Menem).

Massive privatisation of broadcasting began following the victory of Carlos Menem in 1989. With little opposition from private media owners, President Menem sold two government-owned TV stations in Buenos Aires. Channel 11 was bought by Televisora Federal (TELEFE), and Channel 13 was bought by Arte Radiotelevisivo Argentino, as part of a general process of privatisation of the public sector. The new owners were part of the growing Argentine multimedia industries. The new owners of Channel 11, TELEFE, own the Atlántida publishing company. They also own Radio Continental (AM and FM), a local cable TV system in La Plata, and a local TV channel, radio station, and newspaper (*La Nueva Provincia*) in Bahía Blanca. The owners of Channel 13, Arte Radiotelevisivo Argentino, are the owners of the newspaper *Clarín* and of radio and television channels in the interior of the country. *Clarín* owners also have ownership in the newsprint industry, Papel Prensa, and in Radio Mitre AM and FM 100, and the news agency DYN, as well as extensive holdings in real estate (Raffo 1992).

ATC was the only remaining state-owned national television network. In 1992, the channel established agreements with Televisa, the Mexican media conglomerate, to produce programming, and with PROTELE, a Los Angeles-based Televisa company, for the exclusive foreign distribution and sales of ATC programming. In a further move toward privatisation, in January 1993 President Menem signed a decree establishing TV Channel 4, dedicated to non-commercial cultural programmes, replacing government-owned TV Channel 7 ATC. Channel 4, the new government TV channel, will start broadcasting as soon as ATC is privatised.

The expansion of cable

The Argentine market is the largest and most profitable cable market in Latin America. There are presently an estimated 1,000 cable systems in Argentina offering viewers an average of 30 channels. The number of subscribers is growing at about 40 per cent per year. Four local Argentine news services are already on the air as pay-TV services: Telenoticias, Cablevision, La Red, and TV Cronica, all competing with CNN, ECO and NBC News. Cable television development in Argentina is the largest in Latin America.[4] Cable systems now provide services to wide expanses of the country, formerly served only by local stations that purchased and re-broadcast programming from one of the large capital city channels.[5] The

---

3   Channel 2 was later sold. The new owners of Channel 2 also own Cablevisión, Radio América, FM Aspen, FM Sport, and the newspaper *El Cronista Comercial*.

4   Cable television began as a supplement to the over-the-air system in those locations where geography made reception impossible. Community antennas linked to small cable systems provided services in these areas, re-broadcasting signals from the capital city channels. Community systems, consisting of a satellite antenna and a small cable network, multiplied after 1982 when ATC began nationwide satellite transmission. Although they could not function as networks, the provincial TV stations purchased their programming from the capital-city stations, the only stations with sufficient resources to produce their own programming. Most provincial stations operated in monopoly markets. Without cable, 70 per cent of the population of the country would have access to only one channel, 12 per cent would have access to two channels, and 18 per cent to more than two channels.

5   Most of the growth in Argentine television in the last 15 or so years has been in relay stations rather than in local channels originating programming.

Year	Originating Channels	Relay Channels
1974	35	39
1983	40	132
1987	41	299
1990	41	384

exponential growth of cable television in Argentina, compared to its relatively slower growth in Brazil and Mexico, is directly linked to the use of satellites. The cable systems in the interior of the country offer ten to twelve satellite channels, in addition to the over-the-air private channels from Buenos Aires. The Argentine Association of Cable Television estimates that three million households are connected to cable, of which 360,000 are located in Buenos Aires (served by Cablevisión, VCC, and three smaller systems: Video Cable Privado, Buenos Aires Cable, and Multicanal). Cablevisión and VCC have diversified since the days when they offered mainly films and mini-series. They now offer channels for women and children and foreign channels which they transmit directly or via delayed signal.

Media's new political power

Analysts (Zuleta-Puceiro 1993) have observed that Argentine politicians, unlike their counterparts in Brazil, historically lack their own media or close ties to media or print publishers. Historically, this situation has been more the decision of media owners than of politicians. Private media, accustomed to Argentina's perennial political instability, prefer to be close to the seat of power, whatever it may be, avoiding permanent commitments and, in times of trouble, bunkering down and waiting for more favourable conditions. With the return of democratically elected governments, this situation has made the broadcast media slightly more powerful than the relatively weak Argentine political parties. As a result, the mass media remain virtually unregulated, and the political parties and democratic institutions too weak to impose regulations.

Until recently, because of the absence of monopolies and oligopolies in television ownership, the Argentine media, like those of Colombia, were fragmented. There were no national TV networks, strong multimedia groups, or political 'padrinos' for the Argentine media, leading one analyst to observe, 'The possibility of an Argentine candidate being created primarily by television exposure is at present unthinkable.' (Zuleta-Puceiro 1993) This possibility, however, may not be so distant. The Argentine media are becoming increasingly centralised and acquiring monopoly control of media markets. This is the result of the privatisation of the state-owned TV stations, a ruling allowing newspaper companies to own broadcasting media, and the elimination of the prohibition on networks and the limitation on the number of TV licenses that can be owned by one individual.

At the same time, the media's political power is growing. A recent study of the role of the mass media in the rise of political scandals in Menem's Argentina points to the growing centrality of the mass media in Argentine politics.

> Democratic continuity, institutional inertia, and the emergence of newspapers more adversarial to the government amidst dramatically better conditions for press freedom, are key processes in the proliferation of political exposes and the creation of a denunciation-charged climate. These developments prepared the way for the mass media to consolidate an extraordinary, central, and new role in Argentine political communication and in the country's democracy (Silvio Waisbord 1992, 28).

The inability or unwillingness of the Argentine Government to pass new legislation limiting media concentration and cross ownership point to a continuation of the power of the new Argentine media conglomerates, for the first time, however, perhaps pared up against democratic institutions which are also growing in strength.

9
Uruguay

U ruguay and Chile experienced long periods of democratic rule through most of the 20th century. In Uruguay, this tradition was interrupted by 12 years of military rule from 1973 to 1985. In Chile, the military were in power from 1973 to 1990. In both countries, domestic broadcasting policies before the dictatorships were a basic part of the democratic give and take of the societies, with different interests competing for control of broadcasting and no single monopolistic media industry developing. In Chile the fragmentation of the broadcasting industry was fundamentally the result of the compromise decision among the different political parties to place television channels under the administration of state and church-run universities. In Uruguay it was the result of competition among different radio and television station owners, none of which were directly linked to the state or to a particular government or political party, which occurred within a democratic system.

In both Uruguay and Chile, the competition among different interests in broadcasting ended with the gradual breakdown of democracy and, in 1973, with brutal military take-overs of the government. For over a decade in Uruguay and for even longer in Chile, the military kept the media under strict control and censorship, while, at the same time, allowing for their commercial growth in commercially competitive domestic markets. Neither dictatorship, however, was able to forge a close political relationship with a private domestic broadcaster, as was the case in Brazil and Mexico, and which led to the formation in these countries of monopolistic domestic broadcasting industries.

Government censorship of broadcasting was lifted with the return to democracy in Uruguay and Chile, and both societies struggled to forge new domestic broadcasting policies under democratically elected governments. At the same time, they witnessed the rapid growth of commercial broadcasters and their consolidation with other domestic media like newspapers and cable TV. In Chile this growth and consolidation is occurring in an environment of considerable foreign investment. In Uruguay, it is mainly a case of domestic media concentration. Both countries must deal with the continued legacy of the military's power in government and, indirectly, in the media, although this is more a problem in Chile than it is in Uruguay.

Uruguayan broadcasting, too late for the welfare state

When radio broadcasting began in the early 1920s, small, relatively affluent Uruguay, lodged between Brazil and Argentina, had many of the characteristics of a modern welfare state. Uruguay had a prosperous economy, based mainly on exports of agriculture and livestock, although most of its population of two million inhabitants lived in urban areas, 30 per cent of them in Montevideo, the capital city. Through much of the first half of the 20th century, the Uruguayan population enjoyed political stability, social justice, a collective presidential regime, and high levels of health care, education, and social security.

Between 1900 and 1933 under President Jose Batlle y Ordonez, a political élite transformed the Uruguayan state into a powerful economic and social actor. Batlle's government nationalised foreign enterprises and created a strong state presence in the economy. The Batlle reforms affected banking, utilities, meat packing, transportation, telephone and postal services, and many other areas. Until as late as 1929, however, they did not include the establishment of a public or state broadcasting services. Meanwhile, Uruguayan commercial radio flourished. Most of the first Uruguayan radio stations obtained their precarious and easily revocable operating licenses by executive decree. In 1929 the Uruguayan government created the Servicio Oficial de Difusion Radio Electrica SODRE. In addition to broadcasting, the state-owned company included a national symphony orchestra, a national ballet, and a film club. The state-owned radio station, however, was one among many other Uruguayan radio stations, most of which were commercial.

Uruguay's economic prosperity enabled private radio stations and newspapers to build up audiences attractive to advertisers and operate without state subsidies. The Uruguayan media experienced none of the direct or indirect state subsidies that enabled large private monopolies to grow in Mexico or Brazil. More importantly, the stable political climate made it unnecessary for the government to interfere in the operations or content of the private media. The only law directly regulating Uruguayan broadcasting (Law 8,390) was enacted in 1928 and addressed the use of the broadcasting spectrum. By this time, radio frequencies were allocated by the Dirección de los Servicios de Radio-Comunicaciones, occasionally in consultation with the Ministry of Education, and not by the executive.

The introduction of television

When television began in 1955 the Uruguay's economic prosperity was beginning to decline. The growth of domestic industry was thwarted by the small size of the Uruguayan consumer market; traditional export markets were closing, and the traditional agricultural export sector had not been modernised since the turn of the century. The government authorised three commercial TV channels, initially in association with the three US television networks. The first commercial channel, Saeta TV, Channel 10 began broadcasting in 1956. Four years later the second channel, Montecarlo TV Channel 4, went on the air. It was followed in 1962 by the third channel, Teledoce Channel 12. A SODRE-owned government channel joined the three commercial stations in 1963. The four television channels were regulated under the 1928 broadcasting law. For issues of libel, slander, and the right of reply, broadcasting was placed under the National Press Law of 1935.

Early on Uruguayan private broadcasters were able to thwart the development of any serious competition from the public or state-owned broadcasting sector. The operations of SODRE's Channel 5 were modest in scope. The state channel primarily aired reruns of movies. In 1964 new legislation authorised both public and private advertising on the state-operated channel, and the national budget set aside 20 per cent of all public sector advertising for SODRE. Government advertising was unable to cover the cost of SODRE's programming goals, however, and the next year the channel was opened to commercial as well as government advertising.

The Uruguayan National Association of Broadcasters, ANDEBU, contested the new regulation permitting SODRE to accept commercial advertising. The members of ANDEBU accused the government of unfair competition and of violating the Uruguayan Constitution. In response, Uruguayan politicians cited the long national tradition of public service and state ownership in other areas of the economy. They argued in favour of a public monopoly of broadcasting for Uruguay, based on a European public broadcasting model. Despite the opposition of many members of parliament, the ANDEBU position carried the day, and thereafter no commercial advertising was allowed on the SODRE TV channel.

The initiation of authoritarianism

By the mid-1960s the political and economic cycle that had fostered Uruguay's welfare state and prosperous economy was coming to an end. The Uruguayan economy, chronically dependent on agricultural exports, had weakened as a results of shifts in world food markets and prices. The national economy stagnated and inflation rose, causing growing poverty and social conflict. The Uruguayan government became increasingly centralised and authoritarian in order to deal with the growing social unrest that accompanied Uruguay's economic decline. These tendencies were heightened by the threat of the Tupamaros guerrilla movement and changes in the traditional two-party system with the emergence of a left-wing coalition movement. The Uruguayan Constitution was changed, reintroducing a strong one-person presidential regime. The executive branch, now controlled by the armed forces, slowly moved towards a dictatorship. The military's role increased in 1972 with legal powers given them by parliament's declaration of a state of internal war in the country.

The mass media soon began to feel the effects of authoritarianism. In 1967, beginning with the newspaper *Epoca*, the government routinely censored and shut down newspapers and magazines. Radio, television, and newspapers were forced to adopt to the new political controls. In some cases the media became silent partners of the regime, docilely obeying government censorship, manipulating information and distorting the news. In other cases, media owners resisted self-censorship and they were often jailed and their newspapers and stations were shut down.

The media under authoritarianism

In 1973 the Uruguayan military openly assumed control of the government and dismissed the national parliament. They ruled the country for the next 12 years, systematically destroying the judicial system, the political parties, and all independent forms of information or cultural expression including universities, labour unions, sports clubs, and the media. After 1973 Uruguay had no political parties, no parliament, no independent judiciary system, and no independent newspapers or media. The military exercised complete ideological control over schools, books, theatres, and even community cultural centres. The military regime remedied few if any of Uruguay's chronic social and economic problems. By raising the defence budget to 40 per cent of the national budget and later opening the borders to speculative international capital and consumer goods, they made many problems worse (Faraone 1987).

The Uruguayan military traditionally had operated as a separate organisation, isolated from much of Uruguayan society. They were inexperienced and unprepared for rule. Once in charge of the country, the military did not build a government of alliances with right-wing political or economic groups, or with the media. The Uruguayan military's faltering economic policies zig-zagged between state intervention and laissez-faire (Rama 1985). Probably as a result of the military's lack of ties with domestic political and economic groups, the regime paid more attention to setting up their own propaganda machine and controlling the news in newspapers, magazines, and radio and television stations than in building up a strong private broadcasting industry allied to their cause, as was the case with Globo and the military in neighbouring Brazil.

In 1974 the Uruguayan military regime set up the National Administration of Telecommunications, ANTEL. The military placed the telephone and broadcasting services, previously administered by the state-owned power and telephone company, UTE, under the new organisation. State-owned radio and television broadcasting remained under ANTEL until 1984. That year, a month before the elections that would return the country to a civilian administration, the military transferred the administration of broadcasting to the Ministry of Defence. For ten years under military rule, ANTEL controlled the distribution of radio and television frequencies and all technical and operational aspects of Uruguayan broadcasting. It licensed and regulated domestic and international news agencies and supervised the installation of telecommunications equipment and infrastructure. ANTEL, however, could not grant broadcasting licenses. (The military retained the authority to distribute licenses.)

In 1978, the military enacted a new broadcasting decree that defined broadcasting services as public services that could be exploited by both official and private bodies. The law gave preference to the official broadcasting services of SODRE in terms of allocation of frequencies and the location of stations. It established penalties and punishments for the private stations that transmitted without government authorisation or violated any of their licensing conditions. The decree also fixed penalties for transmissions that disturbed the peace, discredited morality and good manners, threatened national security and the public interest, or damaged the national image or reputation of the country. Penalties ranged from warnings to cancelling licenses and shutting down stations permanently and without indemnisation. The National Office of Public Relations of the Presidency was in charge of seeing that all transmission complied with the norms governing communications and opinion.

The military expanded and updated the definition of broadcasting contained in the 1928 law to include all transmissions of sound or pictures destined for direct public reception. Other measures of the dictatorship indirectly affected the media. The regime classified each of its citizens into one of three categories: politically dangerous, neutral, and supporters of the regime. Broadcasters were requested to fire their employees classified as politically dangerous, and many actors, journalists, musicians, and entertainers found themselves unable to work.

Although censorship and ideological control was harsh, the military seldom enforced restrictions on commercial advertising or quotas for national content. Licensees, however, had to take an oath swearing allegiance to the 'democratic republican form of government that governed the country'. No broadcasting licensee could directly or indirectly participate in unpatriotic activities or be involved personally or professionally in any activities that went against the welfare of the country. This broad definition included participation in any political party, all of which were outlawed.

The military added to existing media regulations a list of obligations and requirements for broadcasting content that included morality, good manners, patriotism, nationalism, quality, and respect for the military government and its programme. The National Office of Public Relations of the Presidency monitored the impact of broadcasting content on public opinion. It required that radio and television stations record and save for ten days all news programmes in a foreign language (with translation), and all commentaries, interviews and debates on national and international politics and affairs.

The slow growth of television

The Uruguayan broadcasters were a small, relatively homogeneous group. With the exception of Channel 5 and some small television channels in the interior of the country, about 80 per cent of Uruguayan television was concentrated in three groups. The Romay group owned Channel 4 Montecarlo in Montevideo as well as channels in the interior of the country. The Fontaina de Feo group owned Saeta Channel 10 in Montevideo as well as channels in the interior. The Scheck group owned Teledoce Channel 12 in Montevideo, as well as channels in the interior, Radio Panamericana, two newspapers, and a weekly.

SODRE's Channel 5 captured between 10 and 15 per cent of the television audience, transmitting films, commentaries and cultural and educational materials borrowed from embassies and foreign missions. The remaining 85 to 90 per cent of the television audience was divided more of less equally among the three private capital-city channels and their national networks. The private channels showed mostly imported films and series. There was no attempt by the state to increase national content on Uruguayan television, as occurred in Brazil, or in Argentina under Peron.

Based on the slow growth of television receivers in Uruguay during the military regime, television did not enjoy great popularity. Between 1965 and 1975, the number of television sets grew from 200,000 to 351,000, an increase of 75 per cent. Between 1975 and 1983 under the military, the number rose from 351,000 to 376,000, an increase of only 7 per cent (UNESCO 1985). In 1981, Gallup Uruguay estimated television ownership at about 90 per cent of the households. Television ratings for the same period, however, reveal an audience of only about 25 per cent for men and 30 per cent for women (Castagnola 1981).

The apparent unpopularity of television, however did not appear to concern advertisers. Notwithstanding the slow growth of the television audience, by 1981 Uruguayan television captured 98 per cent of advertising (AUDAP, 1982). In part the increase in TV advertising was the result of the economic policies of the military that opened the Uruguayan economy to a flood of imported goods directed at the upper and upper-middle class consumers.

Uruguayan television was not a sophisticated modern enterprise. Many of the commercial operations of the stations were based on personal relations. Channels owners often exchanged advertising time for products or services. For example, an owner of a television channel who owned a ranch would exchange advertising time on the station for fertiliser for his land. Other owners gave free advertising to insurance companies in exchange for policies covering their employees. Still other stations offered advertising time in exchange for a cut in the profits on the products announced.

The transition to civilian rule

Uruguay's transition to a civilian regime was gradual. The Uruguayan population slowly and painfully recovered their political rights. In 1980 they were able to demonstrate their rejection of the military regime by voting down a referendum for a new military-proposed constitution. In 1982 the military allowed elections to be held within the traditional political parties. National elections were held in 1984, and, in 1985 the first civilian president in over a decade was inaugurated.

On the eve of the presidential elections, the military issued a decree placing the National Direction of Communication under the Ministry of Defence. The military's eleventh hour transfer of broadcasting to the Ministry of Defence created a political problem for the new civilian government. The new Uruguayan Senate unanimously passed a bill returning the National Direction of Communication to ANTEL. The newly elected president, however, openly opposed the bill and lobbied strongly against its passage. Despite the president's opposition, the Chamber of Deputies approved the Senate's bill. The president vetoed the bill, and the two houses were unable to muster the votes necessary to override the veto. The new president, it seemed, was unwilling to challenge the military's control of the communications sector.

Although the military continued to control of the administration of broadcasting, with the return of a civilian regime, the content of radio and television changed significantly. The government abolished many of the military's measures concerning the media along with the most authoritarian sections of the 1978 broadcasting regulations. Newspapers long-banned reappeared on the newsstands, and new and long silenced voices could be heard on radio and TV.

During the transition, television both led and followed the changes in the country. TV owners were anxious not to lose their audiences and to keep up with the political changes that country was undergoing. They sought out previously proscribed political leaders and invited them to participate in their talk shows and newscasts. Even with the return of democracy, however, the military continued to influence television. The military succeeded, for example, in keeping public service announcements from human rights groups off the air during the national debates and the referendum over the prosecution of the members of the armed forces for human rights abuses.

Since the return to democracy, Uruguay has undergone major changes in its economy and workforce, including the development of the service sector, the expansion of the private sector, and the internationalisation of the economy. Cultural changes also are occurring with the introduction of cable TV and satellite delivery systems and the growth of FM radio. As a result of Uruguayan society's increased exposure to different media, the Uruguayan public has become more segmented, active and selective. These changes, under the rebuilt democratic system, will lead to a new accommodation between the broadcasting industry and the country's political leaders.

10 *Chile*

Like Uruguay, the Chilean commercial broadcasting media remained
fragmented and by and large pluralist during most of their initial development under a generally democratic system. In the case of television, this
development occurred relatively late and went on under the management of the
national universities. University ownership of television in Chile reduced the
importance of foreign investment and influence and checked the development of
strong domestic media monopolies. It did not, however, rule out television's commercial growth.

Growing social turmoil and polarisation of Chile's political system in the 1960s,
however, politicised the university channels, destroying the balance between
commercial interests, educational goals of university administrations, and the political parties that had created this compromise. By maintaining strict state control
and ownership of broadcasting, including the university and national television
channels, the sixteen years of dictatorship that followed the coup against Salvador
Allende in 1973 discouraged the growth of powerful domestic media monopolies.
The private broadcasting industry began to grow after 1989 and under democracy,
with the push toward privatisation of government and university-owned television.
Chile's private broadcasting industry, however, is based in part on capital from
Mexico, Venezuela, and Canada. Foreign investment, along with the diversity of
channels and other historical factors, could result in the Chilean broadcasting
media assuming a less direct role in domestic politics than the industry, for
example, of Venezuela or Brazil.

The introduction of television

Chilean television began in 1959, nearly ten years after television's introduction in
most other Latin American countries. The first channels were tucked away in the
Chilean universities; many hoped to shield the new technology from commercial
abuse and political manipulation. A number of factors contributed to the late
arrival of Chilean television. Television technologies were expensive. After the
Korean War a sharp drop on the world market in the price of copper, Chile's main
export, drastically reduced the country's imports. The scarcity of foreign exchange
was compounded in the early 1950s by the protectionist policies pursued by the

Chilean state, severely limiting imports and foreign investment. Commercial television did not fit well with the austere economic policies of Chile's modernising technocrats or with the conservative, 'paternalistic' cultural policies of its traditional political leaders.

The historical weakness of Chilean commercial radio also helps explain the private sector's lack of initiative in the introduction of television. Unlike Brazil and Mexico, Chile did not develop an important national radio industry in the first half of the 20th century. The main Chilean radio chains of the 1940s and 1950s were owned by large agricultural and mining companies: Radio Agricultura by the Sociedad Nacional de Agricultura and Radio Mineria by the Sociedad Nacional de Mineria. Other radio chains formed part of the holdings of different economic groups in insurance, textiles, and livestock. Chile had no multimedia conglomerates; and the domestic media formed part of larger industrial holdings (Catalán 1988).

In the 1950s the Chilean state rebuffed several attempts to set up a private television system. Requests for TV licenses from domestic and foreign companies came under the jurisdiction of the national investment code. The provisions of the code for import substitution, national industrialisation, and high tariffs on foreign imports ruled out foreign investment in broadcasting and made it impossible for Chileans to import the needed equipment to start a television station. In 1956, for example, the Committee of Foreign Investment rejected a request from a US company to set up a television system in Chile and import 30,000 receivers. In turning down the request, the committee argued that television would not stimulate the country's industrial development or improve the exploitation of its national resources (Catalán 1988).

In 1958 in a surprise move, the government suddenly changed its mind about television. Ten days before the inauguration of President Jorge Alessandri, President Carlos Ibañez issued a decree placing television under regulations similar to those governing commercial radio. The new regulations established a system of commercial TV channels in all the main cities and many small local commercial as well as cultural stations. Licenses would be limited to Chilean citizens and required presidential approval as well as the approval of the National Gas and Electricity Company under the Ministry of the Interior. Two-thirds of the TV channels were set aside for commercial use. Educational channels would be established in the main cities, especially those with universities, but could not transmit commercial advertising (Hurtado 1989).

Soon after taking office, President Alessandri crushed the hopes of those who had hoped for the expansion of commercial television. The new president considered television an unnecessary and superfluous investment for a poor country with a high inflation rate and chronic problems of economic stability. Television would dissipate scarce foreign exchange and the limited national savings sorely needed for other areas of development and social welfare. The new president believed in a strong state role in public education. He looked down on mass culture and considered television programming to be mediocre and banal. During his six years in office Alessandri did not award a single commercial television license (Hurtado 1989).

The only portion of the Ibañez television decree that went into effect was that allowing the Chilean universities to set up television stations under their jurisdiction. The university stations went on the air in 1959. No other legislation was enacted regulating the university stations until 1970. Soon after going on the air the university channels violated the only norm governing their operations, that prohibiting the use of commercial advertising.

Chilean universities had a history of public service in the arts and music; they enjoyed intellectual prestige and a reputation for political pluralism. Most importantly, the universities were not identified with the government or with any political party. The university management of television was acceptable to most Chilean political parties. In addition, universities had the technical capacity to experiment with the new medium and a tax-exempt status to import studio and transmission equipment. Local entrepreneurs, however, especially those linked to commercial radio broadcasting and the press, continued unsuccessfully to pressure the Chilean government to allow them to develop private television channels (Catalán 1988).

In 1963 the Chilean university channels increased their broadcasting capacity beyond the initial experimental levels. At that time the private sector made another attempt to enter the domestic television market, arguing that the use of advertising and expansion of coverage by the university stations violated their non-commercial status. Working through congress with the support of a broad political consensus in their favour, however, the university authorities were able to block the private sector's entrance into television (Hurtado 1989).

The parliamentary debates on broadcasting during the initial years of Chilean television reveal a broad political consensus in favour of the university management of television. All the main Chilean political parties: the Christian Democrats, socialists, communists, Radicals and some conservatives, for the most part rejected private commercial television on the grounds that it would favour big business and encourage mass audiences at the expense of educational and cultural programming. Some of the parties in the centre and further to the left feared that commercial television would swing the existing political balance of the media to the right. University-managed television, in fact, was a political stalemate. No one party felt it was at a disadvantage or feared the use of television's power by another party. At a time of growing political conflict in Chile, the pluralism and relative political autonomy of university-managed television were its most important assets (Hurtado and Edwards 1988).

Although the Alessandri administration (1958-1963) limited the expansion of the Chilean university channels, it gave its approval for the universities' use of advertising to finance the channels' operations. Alessandri's successor, Christian Democrat Eduardo Frei (1964-1970), was even stricter than his predecessor in the control of television. Frei closed down up-start regional university channels, blocked the expansion of the university channels in Santiago and the provinces, and refused to extend government credits and subsidies to the university channels. Until as late as 1969, only two Chilean cities, Santiago and Valparaiso, had full television coverage (Hurtado 1989).

The university channels

The three original university channels were located in the Catholic Universities of Santiago and Valparaiso and in the National University of Chile in Santiago. (The

Catholic University of Santiago, despite close ties with the Catholic Church, had government funding and many of its programmes were closely tied to national educational goals.) The Catholic University initiated its television channel in 1959 within its school of engineering. In 1962 the university set up Channel 13 as a separate company, linked to the secretary general and the rector of the university.[1] In 1962 the Vatican gave the university the funds to buy much of the channel's operating equipment. Channel 13, however, was supported largely by commercial advertising. The channel developed separate departments for news, cultural extension, community promotion, and national cultural production. It formed an association with an autonomous commercial company, linked with the US television network ABC, to sell commercial time, produce advertising and programming, and import films and television series, mainly from the United States. By 1964, 30 per cent of Channel 13's programming was imported and, by 1965, nearly half. The channel's pragmatic mix of mass audience programming, advertising, and cultural and educational productions resulted in a financially sound, 'politically correct', and technologically advanced company. Channel 13 also had a social role. It produced special programming for peasants, women, and grassroots organisations and set up teleclubs to discuss programmes with different audience groups.

Channel 9 of the University of Chile was a different story altogether. The University of Chile was traditionally secular, liberal, and public. It defended and represented the educational and cultural goals of many sectors of the Chilean left-wing and centrist parties. Mass commercial advertising and imported US television series were not these sectors' ideas of how to run a university television channel. The university placed the channel within its audiovisual department alongside the film school. At first the channel was run strictly as an educational tool within the programme of basic and high school education of the university's experimental high school. Later, it began to reach out to a larger audience.

In 1965 the tension between the ideals of Channel 9's academic directors and the pragmatism of its artists and technical personnel was resolved with the latter taking control of the channel. Under new management, Channel 9 began to compete with Channel 13 for audiences and advertising and developed a series of high-quality cultural productions and polemic programmes of political analysis and debate. With Channel 13's growing identification with the Christian Democrats, Channel 9 brought in journalists, producers and a public more identified with the left-wing opposition parties. This identification, however, did not keep Channel 9 from using imported TV series to attract mass audiences and advertisers to finance its operations.[2] Despite its change in programming, Channel 9 continued to operate at a deficit and had only about a third as much advertising as Channel 13.

The third university channel, Channel 4 of the Catholic University of Valparaiso, like Channel 9 began in the school of engineering. With strong backing from the university president, the small, provincial university channel imported its first equipment from the United State in 1959. The channel flourished, supported

1   The founding members of the television company were Luis Felipe Letelier, general secretary of the university and national senator; Julio del Rio, the president of RCA Victor in Chile, and Roberto Vergara, ex-minister of Alessandri. Eduardo Tironi, the treasurer of the university, was named its president.

2   Between 1964 and 1965 the percentage of imported programming shown on Channel 9 jumped from 24 per cent to 62 per cent, before settling at about half.

by local business and with the benefit of a captive audience and monopoly market. In addition to locally produced programmes, Channel 4 transmitted programmes purchased from Channels 13 and 9 in Santiago. After 1960 about 60 per cent of the content of Channel 4 was imported, mainly from the United States (Hurtado 1989).

State broadcasting policies

Although the Chilean state defended a policy of non-commercial, public service television, it did not give the universities the subsidies necessary to operate their stations without advertising. In consequence, commercial organisation were set up by the university channels to buy and sell programming and advertising. Chilean television's small audience of about 100,000 sets in 1967, however, hardly competed with films, magazines and newspapers for commercial advertising. Until as late as 1970, the sole legal basis of the three Chilean university channels was Article 24 of the otherwise dead television law of 1958. The operations of the three channels and their use of commercial advertising, programming, and news, functioned entirely outside any national policy. The *de facto* situation of Chilean television developed out of political convenience and compromise. In a highly competitive political environment, it was to every party's advantage to keep the television industry fractured and outside the control of the government or of any one party. The foundations of this comprise began to erode, however, as new actors entered the political arena and a new presidential administration attempted to use television within its overall plan of reform and development (Catalán 1988).

The domestic policy debates that would rock Chilean television for over five years began slowly and quietly. The changes in the television channels were first concealed by the larger political conflict that was going on within the Chilean universities. These conflicts eventually engulfed the entire society and resulted in the breakdown of all democratic institutions. The turmoil in the Chilean universities began during the administration of Christian Democrat President Eduardo Frei. Frei's initially popular administration had run into trouble. Inflation was rising, aggravating labour and social unrest. The Christian Democrats had won the 1964 elections with the help of the right wing, whose support they were losing as a result of their more progressive social policies.

Frei's programme was based on agrarian reform, the nationalisation of national resources including mining, and industrial modernisation. Political support for the Christian Democrats came from the small farmers, the lower-income urban dwellers, the middle class, and the modernising sectors of national industry. The changes and reforms carried out by the Christian Democrats mobilised other sectors of the population that never before had been involved in national politics. Students, grassroots organisations, and labour unions pressured the government for more sweeping reforms and more profound changes in the traditional political and social structure of the country. Strikes, demonstrations and direct political action by these groups were frequent from the mid-1960s on, and pressures for change split the governing party into several factions. Younger members, often more radical than the party leadership, formed splinter parties further to the left (Catalán 1988).

The Chilean university students played an important role in the political movements of the 1960s. Students' first concern was the reform of the academic structure of the university. Student leaders called for more scientific and research
disciplines in the traditional liberal arts curricula and for programmes of community outreach and participation. Community programmes fostered ties between the
traditionally elitist universities and the lower income, economically marginal sectors of Chilean society. Between 1967 and 1968 student movements seized and
occupied all three universities along with their television channels. The original
academic concerns of the student movements spilled over into demands for a larger
role in university government and administration, including student participation
in the university-owned television channels. Despite an increasingly commercial
development and growing independence from university management, the three
university channels were still owned by the universities. It was impossible to shield
the channels from the political movements going on within their walls.

As a result of students protests and occupations of the universities, the government named new university rectors. The new rectors changed the administrative and academic organisations within the universities and hired new personnel,
including that of the television channels.[3] The changes in the universities had
important consequences for the television channels. The first changes were administrative. One of the general objectives of the reforms was to modernise the financial administration of the universities. The directors eliminated much of the
cumbersome bureaucracies of the stations' management and got the stations operating on a financially sound budget, attracting stable sponsorship and reorganising
programming. The administrators of Channel 13 cancelled its agreement with
Protel, its partially US-owned associate in charge of purchasing programming and
selling advertising, and attempted to increase the amounts of domestic content and
bring the channel closer to the life of the university (Hurtado 1989).

As the Chilean universities descended from their ivory tower, the operations of
all three channels became increasingly enmeshed in the complex, culturally and
politically diverse environment of the country. Each channel now represented a different position within the national political spectrum. Channel 4 of Valparaiso tried
to maintain a balanced, politically objective position, particularly during elections.
At Channel 9 in the University of Chile the workers supported the socialist government of Salvador Allende, elected president in 1970. They fought against the
university administrators in order to make the channel more responsive to the
demands of the workers, slum-dwellers and left-wing supporters of the Allende
government. Channel 13 identified with the left-wing positions of the university
and criticised the US role in the Chilean communication media as well as and the
commercialisation of the media in general. The directors of Channel 13 tried to
make university television an educational tool and increase audience participation.

After the university reforms, the labour unions played a stronger role in the
channels than they had in the past. In the Catholic Universities of Santiago and
Valparaiso the workers protested when they considered a programme to be exces-

---

3   The new rectors were members of the Christian Democrat Party. In the Catholic Universities of Santiago and
    Valparaiso the rectors carried out reforms in coordination with centre and left-wing parties. In the University of
    Chile, where the new rector replaced a socialist, the reforms quickly came into conflict with the left-wing students
    and faculty, wanting reforms to move even faster.

sively commercial or representing values offensive to Chilean culture. The labour unions in the University of Chile were affiliated with the communist and extreme left-wing parties. Their negotiating positions in channel management were strong and often came in open conflict with the rector, a Christian Democrat (Mattelart and Piccini 1974).

Up until 1970 the Chilean university television channels had operated virtually without regulation. The university rectors, in association with the faculty, students and workers, had the final and often only say on television's management, content, and political affiliation. Under these conditions of university ownership, and in view of the growing political polarisation of Chilean society, there was little chance for the development of a strong domestic television industry.

The national television channel

As the Christian Democrats neared the end of their administration (1964-1970), it became clear that it would be difficult to win the next elections. The political conditions of the country had changed. Chilean voters had become increasingly polarised between the left and the right, leaving the Christian Democrat centre without a majority. In order to offset their declining popularity and still hoping to be returned to office, in early 1969 the Christian Democrats inaugurated a government television channel. The new channel operated on a nationwide microwave relay network. The Government justified the need for the new state channel on the basis of the educational and cultural conditions of the country and the failure of the university channels to fulfil their educational and cultural missions. The failure of the university channels, the government claimed, was the result of their early commercialisation. The subsidised national channel would be able to successfully deliver culture and education to the masses.

The national channel began operating without any new media law. Fearing they lacked the necessary support to gain congressional approval of the national network and confident they would win support from the provincial politicians once the new system was in place, the government opted for a strategy of *fait accompli*. Once the channel was set up, the Christian Democrats planned to present a law regulating its functioning as well as that of the university channels. The law, however, was presented under radically different circumstances than those originally envisaged by the Christian Democrats. Television Law 17,377 was discussed and approved in the lapse of two weeks that followed the defeat of the Christian Democrats in the 1970 presidential elections, won by to the left-wing Unidad Popular candidate, Salvador Allende (Catalán 1988).

The Chilean television law

The 1970 television law finally gave Chilean television a legal framework. It set up decentralised and multi-party decision-making mechanisms that reduced the power of the president and the channel's director over television management and programming. As originally drafted by the Christian Democrats, the law marked the consolidation of the public service orientation of television and guaranteed the wide representation in the management of Chilean television that had begun with the reforms of the university channels. In its final form, however, passed a few days before Allende became president, the television law became part of the constitutional guarantees negotiated by the right-wing parties and the Christian Democrats in order to allow Allende to take office as president.

The right-wing and the Christian Democrats considered the Allende administration a peril to the political and economic stability of the country. The constitutional guarantees negotiated in order to allow Allende to become president with less than a simple majority of the votes, reduced the power of the executive and set limitations on any possible change in the distribution of power. Under these guarantees, the new television law stopped short of any further reform of the television system and limited any wider social control over Chilean television. Once the Christian Democrats lost the presidency they were willing to shift control of television away from the executive and toward the legislative and judiciary branches of government where they maintained control (Catalán 1988). Fearing the influence of the left-wing parties in the university channels through labour unions and student groups, the law prohibited the university channels from expanding into the provinces and setting up new channels and networks. The university channels were placed under the authority of the university rectors. The council of department heads and other governing organs of the university, controlled by the Christian Democrats, regulated the operations of the channels. By placing the channels under the direction of the university rectors and university authorities, the law reduced the influence of the channels' administrators and of their artistic and technical personnel. This was especially important in the universities in Santiago where reforms had come mainly from the stations' directors and employees.

Paradoxically, while the 1970 television law decreased the political independence of the university channels, it increased their economic independence. For the first time in the history of Chilean television, the university channels received funds from the national budget. The law gave the universities technical and economic assistance to fulfil their educational and cultural objectives and authorised their long-established but illegal use of commercial advertising. Public funds allowed the university channels to build new studios, acquire equipment, and increase their transmission time.

The national channel under President Allende

The new law stated that the national channel was a public channel and could not be subject to manipulation by the government in office. According to law, the director of the national channel was named by the president and subject to parliamentary approval. Because parliament was controlled by the opposition, not all the channel's directors under Allende supported his administration. Members of the Christian Democrat Party controlled the employees' union of the national channel during the Allende administration, their jobs secured by the constitutional guarantees. In the struggle for the control of the national channel, the left-wing parties fought to maintain control over certain strategic programmes like news and information shows.

Under these limitations, Allende was never able to put into place a coherent national broadcasting policy. Chilean television became caught up in the larger conflicts of Chilean society. The initial objectives of the broadcasting policies of the

Allende administration such as increased domestic content, grassroots participation, and cultural diversity, fell by the wayside in the bitter struggle for the ideological and political control of the medium. The ability of Allende's left-wing coalition to include television in their wider social reforms was sharply restricted by the constitutional guarantees negotiated with the right-wing and Christian Democrat opposition. The guarantees had shifted control of the national and university television channels toward the legislative and judicial branches and the higher administrative bodies of the university where the supporters of the Allende administration never held or soon lost control. The freeze on firing personnel often meant that pro-reform directors were unable to carry out their programmes because of the opposition of their staff (Catalán 1988).

Despite government funding for television after 1970, Chilean television was not able to increase national productions or lower the proportion of imported US films and series. With the exception of Channel 13, during the Allende administration the other channels actually increased the amount of foreign, mainly US programming.[4] Advertising from domestic and foreign industries played an important role in this development in Chilean broadcasting. Between 1967 and 1970, the university channels had depended on commercial advertising. Domestic and foreign firms distributed their advertising to those channels supporting the private sector. The channels that appeared to favour political change and socialist economic policies saw their advertising share dwindle. Channels 9, 4, and 13 all experienced sharp drops in advertising in the pre-electoral period of 1970. Under Allende, advertising from the nationalised state-owned industries partially offset the loss of advertising from the private sector.[5]

Chilean broadcasting under the military

The military coup that overthrew Salvador Allende on 11 September 1973 put an abrupt and brutal end to the debates and struggles over Chilean broadcasting. In the years that followed, the authoritarian politics and economic liberalism of the military dictatorship converted Chilean television into a strictly commercial enterprise under close ideological control and government censorship. Although television stations remained within the universities, the military authorities severed all links between the channels and other groups within the universities or the community. Television advertising jumped, as did the proportion of foreign films and

---

4   Foreign programming on Channel 4 rose from about 63 per cent before 1968 to about 67 per cent after 1968; Channel 9 from about 45 per cent before 1968 to about 47 per cent after 1968. Foreign programming on Channel 13 remained the same at about 52 per cent, and Channel 7 began operations in 1970 with about 50 per cent foreign programming (Hurtado 1988).

5   Advertising and the clients were important considerations for Chilean television. Despite social service orientations, television was a relatively elitist medium in Chile. In 1968 there were only 174,000 television receivers in the country. By 1973 there were a million sets for a population of about ten million. Television viewers came mainly from the middle and upper classes making up about 40 per cent of the Chilean population. Their income and education levels strongly influenced their viewing habits and tastes in music and entertainment. This did not occur with radio where Radio Portales, a supporter of the United Popular government of Allende, run by radio professionals, maintained its traditional leadership in audiences, especially among the lower income sectors. Its audience leadership held despite aggressive and well financed campaigns to attract listeners by the opposition and right-wing radios, Radio Balmaceda of the Christian Democrats and Radio Agricultura of the National Party. The programmes of other left-wing radio stations, Corporacion of the socialist party and Magallanes of the communist party, however, failed to attract large audiences. Their directors were unable to make their political and ideological messages attractive to mass audiences (Munizaga and de la Maza 1979).

series. The sophisticated technology and nationwide infrastructure of the national channel was placed at the service of a totalitarian regime supported by a small economic and political elite (Munizaga 1982).

One of the first measures of the Agusto Pinochet regime was to dissolve all the left-wing parties and take control of their property and assets and those of their members and sympathisers. With this measure a large portion of the Chilean mass media immediately fell under the control of the dictatorship. The military issued a Law of National Security and related decrees that censored and strictly controlled all the media that remained in private hands. The regime placed military directors in the university television channels and closed down and censored radio stations throughout the country. (As many as 40 journalists were killed during and after the coup and many others lost their jobs and went into exile.)

The free market economic policies of the Pinochet regime and the withdrawal of state subsidies exposed the Chilean media to foreign competition for the first time. Unlike the Brazilian military, The Chilean military made little effort to protect national culture or use nationalist themes. Under its free market policy the Chilean military moved to make the government-owned media – the national television network, the national film industry, the government publishing house – financially self-sufficient (Fuenzalida 1983). The withdrawal of state subsidies and the drive toward economic self-sufficiency meant that television had to fill most of its time with cheaper foreign series.[6] Many of those Chilean television and film producers who were not forced into exile made TV commercials in order to survive (Hurtado 1988).

In addition to the 'privatisation' of television, the Pinochet regime removed all political debate from the television screen. Political debate and discussions were not permitted on television until 1988. That year, during a national plebiscite on the military's continuation in power, the opposition coalition of political parties was allotted 15 minutes daily to make their case to the voters to vote against the military's proposal to remain in office. The opposition's strategy, planned through the use of focus groups and sophisticated production techniques, was successful. The military's bid to stay in power failed, and, one year later, free presidential elections were held for the first time in almost twenty years (Hirmas 1992).

Private, commercial and international under democracy

The Partnership of Parties for Democracy (Concertacion de Partidos por la Democracia), the winner of the 14 December 1989 national presidential elections, consisted of seventeen parties.[7] The Partnership chose a single presidential candidate, Patricio Aylwin, to run in the presidential election against the candidate of the military government. The Partnership's platform on television proposed to:

---

6 By 1979, 71.2 per cent of Chilean television programming was imported, up from 55 per cent in 1973 (Hurtado 1988).

7 The Christian Democrats, three socialist parties, the Humanist Party, the Radical Party, the Radical Democratic Socialist Party, the Christian Left Party, the MAPU, the Greens, the Social Democrat Party, and Centre Alliance Party, the Party for Democracy and three others.

- Review existing television laws following a national debate, discussion and approval by the democratically elected parliament.
- Guarantee freedom of expression and creation and equal access to television by different political opinions and cultural groups.
- Ensure the allocation of the radio frequency spectrum to fully benefit Chilean society.
- Maintain the National Television Network and the university channels, ensuring their autonomy from the government.
- Establish mechanisms to guarantee social objectives, in the event the electorate votes to award new licenses to the private sector.
- Promote the decentralisation of the television system through the creation of local stations.
- Encourage independent national productions, employment of Chilean artists and technicians and Chilean television exports.
- Regulate the quantity and quality of advertising and seek other sources of financing for programmes of high cultural and social interest.

The position on television of the Coalition Democracy and Progress (Democracia y Progreso) – the loser in the December elections – as expressed by presidential candidate Hernan Buchi, opposed any public supervision of the mass media and any direct or indirect official information policy. The Coalition objected to any form of supervision of the media under any pretext: ethical, moral, social, or economic. The Coalition's 'Program for a Government of National Renovation', however, expressed the need to exercise some control over television content. The programme would place television on neutral ground by establishing the autonomy of the National Channel with an independent directory composed of freely elected individuals with high standings in their fields. It also called for private channels and an autonomous National Television Council with the power to insure programming did not harm 'the cultural and spiritual formation the young receive in the family and school'. The programme explicitly criticised state-university television for its 'poor quality programming and the presence of widely disseminated, generally foreign values'.

With the return to democracy under President Aylwin, Chilean broadcasting has seen the introduction of successful new private commercial television stations, the growth of cable TV, and the shift of the national television station in the direction of wider 'public' rather than 'government' control. The legislation enacted under Pinochet has been discarded and a new telecommunications law is being drafted, along with changes in copyright regulations. Chile's strong economic growth, averaging about seven per cent over the last several years, has made broadcasting a very lucrative business.

Democracy also brought with it the entrance of foreign capital in Chilean television in Channel 9, Megavisión, a new private channel owned by business magnate Ricardo Claro and Mexico's Televisa, that reaches 85 per cent of Chile's television households with a majority of imported programmes from the United States and Mexico. The Claro group also owns some radio stations, magazines, and, in partnership with the US TCI, Metropolis, a cable company. Channel 11 of the University of Chile is now part-owned (49%) by Venezuela's media conglomerate Venevision. La Red, another new private channel, is 50 per cent owned by the print company COPESA and 50 per cent owned by CanWest, a Winnipeg based Canadian broadcaster. Valparaiso also has a new private local channel.

Radio remains more pluralist, owned by labour unions, private enterprises, the Church, different political parties, and non-profit and community organisations. As of March 1993, there were 654 radio stations in Chile, of which 483 were FM and 171 AM. The vast majority of these stations are very small; almost two-thirds are under 1 KW. Most of the lower powered stations are located in the provinces, while the larger stations serve the main cities and their surrounding areas. Some of larger capital city stations are expanding throughout the country with affiliates, for example, the Compania Radio Chilena (Radio Chilena AM and Aurora and Galaxia FM) took over the formerly government-owned radio stations in Talca and Concepción and is expanding its network to Antofagasta, Copiapo, and La Serena. The expansion of Chilean radio is not limited by national borders. The Chilean radio company Enchique-Warner, owner of five stations in the north, has recently installed an affiliate in Buenos Aires.

For the most part Chile does not demonstrate the patterns of cross-ownership of radio and television so prevalent in other countries of Latin America It does, however, in cable. In addition to the Claro purchase of Metropolis, the Chilean Telecom Company (CTC) has purchased a majority stake in the cable company Intercom from the Edwards family, owners of *El Mercurio*. In 1995, Chile had 25 cable companies providing some type of pay-per-view service for about half a million subscribers. Three of these companies, however, accounted for almost 98 per cent of the cable subscriptions, and two of the big three companies had announced their merger for 1996.

Notwithstanding the entrance of foreign investment, and the growth of telephone-cable multimedia groups, the historic inability of the Chilean state to form a strong alliance with a private broadcasting monopoly, probably will result in a weaker and less protagonist role of the Chilean media in domestic politics as the country continues along the road to democracy.

Conclusion

This book presents a picture of how radio and television broadcasting developed in Latin America and the foreign and domestic forces that helped to shape the industries and their relations with the state and other actors. This picture confirms the importance of the US broadcasting industry and the actions of the US Government during the early development and growth of Latin American broadcasting. Domestic forces, however, are seen to have played an even stronger role in shaping the evolution of radio and later television in the region. Foreign capital, technology, and influence were present in the broadcasting industries of all the Latin American countries. In every country, however, different broadcasting industries emerged as a result of the political and economic forces operating in each society. In the development of Latin American broadcasting, the nature of the state and of the state-society relations, the legitimacy of governments, and the organisational strengths and legacies of leadership played a more crucial role than international relations.

The conflicts over the control of the economic and political benefits of the broadcasting industries, and the agreements and accommodations reached by different domestic actors, described in the eight national chapters, largely defined the way radio and television developed in the countries of Latin America. This domestic dimension was the interface or mediator between the international forces described in chapter one and local markets and audiences. When the mediator was a powerful authoritarian state with weak organs of political representation and participation, as was the case of Mexico and Brazil, monopolistic broadcasting industries developed that displayed little political – or economic – independence from the state. In these cases, the broadcasting media did not challenge the ruling parties and largely ignored any role as watchdog or public service. In turn, they were rewarded by the state with subsidies and little if any regulation on their monopolistic commercial practices. In those societies where the mediator was a weak authoritarian state – with an unstable relationship with the political parties and elites, the case of Peru and Argentina, more fragmented domestic broadcasting industries developed. In these cases, the state was unable to form an alliance with a commercial broadcaster and attempted to form its own broadcasting institutions. These, however, failed, as a result of the political downfall of their creators and the lack of support from domestic entrepreneurs.

In more democratic societies, the case of Colombia and Venezuela under two-party rule, two or three strong domestic broadcasting industries developed that often were played out one against the other by the competing parties in power.

Here, domestic broadcasting institutions were more subject to regulation and state oversight, and their public service and watchdog roles were more important than were those of broadcasting in countries with less democratic political systems. The most pluralist and democratic media institutions in the region developed in those countries that enjoyed long traditions of multi-party democratic rule – Uruguay and Chile. Although both countries suffered under dictatorships for more than ten years, their military rulers were unable to form an alliance with a domestic media industry and resorted to censorship and harsher forms of control and manipulation of radio and television. During the periods of dictatorship in these two countries, domestic broadcasting remained fragmented, although it benefited at times from the economic policies of the military. With the return of democratically elected governments in Uruguay and Chile, domestic media have regained their previous independence in competitive markets, in the case of Chile with the presence of significant foreign investment.

Some conclusions need to be drawn from the history of broadcasting in Latin America. One is the key role of the United States Government and industry in determining the initial character of Latin American broadcasting. It would have been almost impossible for state-owned or operated radio and television to survive on a large scale in Latin American in the face of the pressures and inducements of US capital, industries and government. Another is that once the commercial nature of Latin American broadcasting was established, i.e. that the media would be operated for profit and financed by advertising, the nature of the industry that evolved was a result of the domestic forces at work in each country. In other words, private commercial media is not the same as democratic media. In those countries under non-democratic regimes, the media developed in a highly monopolistic fashion, ignoring any public service or watchdog function. In countries under democratic rule, private commercial broadcasting was subject to regulation in the public interest and developed in a more competitive environment.

These conclusions are neither an apology nor a negation of the influence of foreign models and interests on Latin American broadcasting and especially television. Latin American broadcasting did not evolve in a hothouse; it was exposed to foreign capital, technology, and influence from its earliest days and it grew quickly to operate in an international environment. These conclusions do, however, have theoretical as well as applied implications for the study of international communications and national communication policies.

Theoretically, they suggests that the type of nation state and what goes on in its interior is a key factor to be considered in the overall impact of international communications. Cultural imperialism is not simply the impact of one nation state on an abstract notion of another nation state. The influence of US television on China is very different from its influence on France. It is not the same in a Chile under Pinochet as it is in a Chile under democracy. What goes on in the interior of a country matters in terms of how foreign influences will be received and 'mediated.'

Applied to policy, these conclusions suggest that actions by a foreign state or industry are not the sole or even the principal cause of the failure of many Latin American societies to develop democratic and participatory domestic media. Often, national communication policies are dictated more by interests of political survival and control than by concern with access, balance, 'national content,' or free competition. Nationalist solutions to 'cultural dependency' like quotas on domestic content mean little without the development of open, competitive, domestic communication systems.

The growth of powerful domestic media monopolies in Latin America was not inevitable. National-level politics, the types of party structures, and the democratic and representative nature of domestic institutions led to what type of broadcasting media developed in each country. Because these relationships, structures, and institutions largely excluded the broader demands of civil society and responded to the more immediate demands for political survival of their rulers, in many countries the broadcasting systems that emerged were largely monopolistic and operated outside any democratic political framework.

In those cases where an authoritarian state reached an accommodation with a domestic industry, a strong, monopolistic and increasingly politically autonomous broadcasting industry emerged. In countries where this accommodation was not achieved, domestic industries remained fragmented until political conditions evolved. Liberal international systems helped foster authoritarian national media structures when they met with an authoritarian state and no domestic political opposition. In countries with democratic systems, these same forces increased competition on the domestic markets. Most countries of Latin America received the impact of international broadcasting industries without strong democratic traditions, however, and while in the process of undergoing increasing political instability and authoritarianism.

If the government was able to 'trust' the national media, these prospered, a prosperity that was more conducive to economic gain than it was to democracy or the 'free market place of ideas'. This was the case of Mexico, Brazil, and, to some degree, Venezuela. If a domestic accommodation between the media and the state did not occur, as was the case of Peru and Argentina, the domestic media, although commercially operated, failed to produce a monopolistic structure. In these instances where political power remained fragmented no strong domestic media monopoly emerged as long as the state deliberately (Colombia) or randomly (Argentina) parceled out the media among different forces.

In Chile and Uruguay, monopolistic, undemocratic broadcasting did not develop. In Chile this originally was due to the political compromise of placing the television channels under the administration of the universities. In Uruguay it was the result of competition among different media groups, none of which were directly linked to the state or to a particular government. The give and take among different interests in broadcasting ended with the gradual breakdown of democracy and, in 1973, with brutal military take-overs in both countries, but is resuming today.

The domestic relationships of broadcasting in Latin America are continuously renegotiated. Most theories of international relations, however – realist, liberal and Marxist – in different ways ignore this domestic space of renegotiation. Realist theories are unable to recognise differences among or within states at different periods. Liberal theory ignores that free markets do not guarantee democracy or the open market place of ideas when faced with domestic authoritarianism. Marxist theory, especially of imperialism, ignores the conflicts and alliances that occur in the interior of a society in response to foreign influence and power.

Because these theories failed to 'integrate' this space of domestic mediation, they have no framework in which to analyse national communications policies and institutions.[1] This book hopes to have made a contribution to building such a framework.

---

1   Hamid Mowlana points out this failure in his study of Global Information and World Communication:

   Among many writers on Third World development and communication there is not only no deep consciousness about the nature of change independent from big-power politics, but there is little consensus as to the nature and direction of indigenous cultural revolution or evolution now taking place ... The failure of many students of international relations and international communications ... to predict the social, cultural, and political development of many parts of the world in the last ten years is a case in point (1986, 201).

References

Agudo Freites, Raúl. 1976. *La Reglamentación Legal de la Comunicación en Venezuela*. Caracas: UCV.

Alemán Velasco, Miguel. 1976. El Estado y la Televisión. *Nueva Política*, No. 3. Vol 1.

Alfonso, Alejandro. 1985. Politicas Comunicaciones: experiencias de una Decada en Venezuela. *Chasqui*, No. 14, Abril-Junio, 1985, Quito, Ecuador.

Amaral, Roberto and Cesar Guimaraes. 1994. Media Monopoly in Brazil. *Journal of Communication* 44(4) Autumn. 26-38.

Anuario de la Camera Nacional de la Industria de Radio y Televisión. 1971. Mexico City.

AUDUP. 1982. *Uruguay '82, Estadisticas Nacionales*

Barnouw, Erik. 1970. *The Golden Web: A History of Broadcasting in the United States*, Volume II, 1933-1953.

Beltrán, Luis Ramiro and Elizabeth Fox. 1980. *Comunicacion dominada: los Estados Unidos en los medios de América Latina*. Mexico: Nueva Imagen.

Blanchard, Margaret. 1986. *Exporting the First Amendment the Press and Government Crusade of 1945-1952*. New York: Longman.

Boyd, Douglas. 1974. The Pre-History of the Voice of America: US Shortwave Broadcasting to 1942. *Public Telecommunications Review*. Vol. 2 No. 6 (December) 38-45.

Bruce, Gregory. 1970. *The Broadcasting Service, An Administrative History*, United States Information Agency Special Monograph Series, No. 1, Washington: USIA.

Brunner, Jose Joaquin, Carlos Catalan and Alicia Barrios. 1989. Chile: Transformaciones culturales y conflictos de la modernidad. In *Hacia un nuevo orden estatal en America Latina? Innovación cultural y actores socio-culturales*, ed CLACSO, 33-161. Buenos Aires: CLACSO.

Caletti Kaplan, Ruben Sergio. 1988. Communication Policies in Mexico: An Historical Paradox of Words and Actions. In *Media and Politics in Latin America: The Struggle for Democracy*. ed. Elizabeth Fox, London: Sage.

Camera de Diputados. 1977. Proceso Legislativa de la Reforma Política, Iniciativa y Proyecto de Decreto. *Compilación de Diario de los Debates*.

Canclini, Nestor Garcia. 1982. *Las culturas populares en el capitalism*. México: Nueva Imagen.

Canclini, Nestor Garcia. 1977. *Arte popular y sociedad en América Latina*, México, Grijalbo.

Caparelli, Sergio. 1986. *Comunicaco de Massa sem Massa*. São Paulo: Summus, 3rd, ed.

Capriles, Oswaldo. 1980. *El estado y los medios de comunicación en Venezuela*. Caracas: ININCO.

Cardoso, Fernando Henrique and Enzo Faletto. 1979. *Dependency and Development in Latin America*. Berkeley: University of California Press.

Castagnola, Jose Luis. 1981. *Comunicación Masiva y Sectores Juveniles*. Montevideo: Centro Latinoamericano de Economía Humana.

Catalán, Carlos. 1988. Mass Media and the Collapse of a Democratic Tradition in Chile. In *Media and Politics in Latin America: the Struggle for Democracy*, 145-55, ed. Elizabeth Fox, London: Sage.

CIESPAL. 1967. *Dos semanas de la prensa en America Latina*. Quito: CIESPAL.

Cohn, Gabriel. 1971. *Comunicao e industria cultural*. São Paulo: Companhia Editora Nacional.

Cohn, Gabriel. 1989. Innovaciones en politicas culturales en Brasil. In *Hacía un nuevo orden estatal en América Latina? Innovación cultural y actores socio-culturales*, ed. CLACSO, 213-239. Buenos Aires: CLACSO.

Colomina de Rivera, Marta. 1968. *El Huesped alienante: un estudio sobre audiencia y efectos de las radio-telenovelas en Venezuela*. Maracaibo: Universidad de Zulia.

Dabrowski, Andrea. 1992. La pegajosa costumbre del ruido y el silencio. *Chasqui*, No. 42.

Darling, Juanita. 1992. Un tigre anda suelto: Televisa se lanza al escenario internacional. *Chasqui*, No. 42, p.14.

Darling, Juanita. 1993. Mexico TV Monopoly Challenged. *The Los Angeles Times*, 29 March.

Dias, Marco Antonio Rodrigues. 1979. Politica de Comunicacion no Brasil. In *Meios de Comunicaco Realidade e Mito*, ed J. Wertein, Rio: Paz e Terra.

Diaz Rangel, Eleazer. 1967. Pueblos subinformados: las agencias de noticias y América Latina. *Cuadernos de Nuestro Tiempo* 3. Universidad Central de Venezuela.

Diehl, Roderick. 1977. South of the Border: the NBC and CBS Networks and the Latin American Venture, 1930-1942. *Communication Quarterly*. 25: 2-12.

Dorfman, Ariel and Armand Mattelart. 1970 *Para leer el Pato Donald: comunicacion de masas y colonialismo*. Buenos Aires: Siglo XXI.

Douglas, George H. 1987. *The Early Days of Radio Broadcasting*. Jefferson NC: McFarland.

Echeverría, Luis. 1974. Opening speech at the Encuentro Mundial de la Comunicacion, 24 October 1974, Acapulco, México.

Esparaza, Luis. 1984. La Política Cultural del Estado Mexicano y el Desarrollo de la TV. *Cuadernos de TICOM*, No. 35, México: UNAM, Xochimilco.

Faraone, Roque. 1987. *De la Prosperidad a la Ruina*. Montevideo: Arca.

Faraone, Roque and Elizabeth Fox. 1988. Communications and Politics in Uruguay. In *Media and Politics in Latin America: the Struggle for Democracy*, 148-156, ed. Elizabeth Fox. London: Sage.

Farias, Luis M. 1981. Public statement, 28 May 1981.

Federico, Maria Elivira Bonavita. 1982. *Historia da comunicacao radio e television no Brasil*. Petropolis: Voces.

Fernandez, Fátima. 1982. *Los Medios de Difusión Masiva en México*, México: Juan Pablos.

Festa, Regina. 1993. Brazilian Cinema Loses its Way. *Media Development*, 1/1993.

Flores Alvarez, Carlos. 1971. *Antena* No. 5, December.

Fox, Elizabeth. 1973. US Television Industry and the Development of Television in Latin America: the Colombian Case. M.A. Thesis, Annenberg School of Communications, University of Pennsylvania.

Francisco, Don, (Francisco, RG 229, Box, 43 'Francisco, Don', USIA Historical Collection)

Fuenzalida, Valerio. 1983. *Transformaciones en la Estructura de la Televisión Chilena*. Santiago: CENECA.

Gargurevich, Juan. 1978. *Prensa, radio y TV: historia crítica*. Lima: Editorial Horizonte.

Gargurevich, Juan. 1990. *Historia de la radio en Perú*. Lima: Horizonte.

Gilpin, Robert. 1987. *The Political Economy of International Relations*. Princeton: Princeton University Press.

Guimaraes, Cesar and Roberto Amaral. 1988. Brazilian Television: A Rapid Conversion to the New Order. In *Media and Politics in Latin America: The Struggle for Democracy*., ed E. Fox, London: Sage.

Gutiérrez Aparacio, Carlos. 1992. Los medios como blancos de guerra. *Chasqui*, No. 42, 39-41.

Herz, D. 1987. *A Historia Secreta da Rede Globo*. Porto Alegre: Tche.

Hills, Jill. 1992. Dependency Theory and Its Relevance Today: International Institutions in Telecommunications and Structural Power. paper presented at the IAMCR Conference, Guaruja, Brazil, August.

Hirmas, Maria Eugenia. 1992. The Chilean Case: Television in the 1988 Plebiscite. In *Television, Politics and the Transition to Democracy in Latin America*, ed. Thomas Skidmore, Washington: The Wilson Center.

History of the Office of the Coordinator of Inter-American Affairs. 1947. A historical report on war administration. Washington: US Government Printing Office.

Hurtado, Maria de la Luz. 1989. *Historia de la televisión en Chile (1958-1973)*. Santiago: CENECA.

Hurtado, Maria de la Luz. 1988. Repression y Innovation under Authoritarianism. In *Media and Politics in Latin America: the Struggle for Democracy*, 103-115, ed. Elizabeth Fox, London: Sage.

Hurtado, Maria de la Luz y Edwards, Paula. 1988. *La Televisión en Chile durante la Democracia: 1959-1973*. Santiago: CENECA.

ININCO. 1977. *Las Política de Comunicación en Venezuela*. Paris: UNESCO.

Jackson, Charles. 1951. 'Private Media and Public Policy,' In *Propaganda in War and Crisis: Materials for American Policy*, ed. Daniel Lerner, New York: George W. Stewart.

Kaplun, Mario. 1973. La comunicación de masas en América Latina. *Educación Hoy* No. 5.

Krasner, Stephen. 1985. *Structural Conflict: The Third World against Global Liberalism*. Berkeley: University of California Press.

Landi, Oscar. 1988. Media, Cultural Process and Political Systems. In *Media and Politics in Latin America*, 138-147, ed. Elizabeth Fox, London: Sage.

Landi, Oscar. 1992. *Devorame Otró Vez: Qué Hizo la Television con la Gente , Que Hace la Gente con la Television*. Buenos Aires, Planeta.

Lerner, Daniel. 1958. *The Passing of Traditional Society*. Glencoe: Free Press.

da Lima, Venecio. 1992. In *Television, Politics and the Transition to Democracy in Latin America*, ed. Thomas E. Skidmore, Washington: The Wilson Centre.

Lopez Portillo, Jose. *Antena*. No. 51, October, 1975.

Lopez Portillo, Jose. 1981. Speech, 14 October in the inauguration of the I Congreso Nacional de Escolaridad y Ejercicio Profesional del Periodismo.

Lowenthal, Abraham. 1975. Peru's Ambiguous Revolution. In *The Peruvian Experiment: Continuity and Change under Military Rule*, ed. A. Lowenthal, pp. 3-43, Princeton: Princeton University Press.

Maculan, Anne Marie. 1981. Proceso decisorio no sector de telecomunicacaos. M.A. IUPERJ.

Martin-Barbero, Jesus. 1987. *De los medios a las mediaciones: Comunicación, cultural y hegemonía*, Barcelona: G.Gili.

Martinez, Hernando. 1978. *Qué es la Televisión?* Bogota: CINEP.

Mattelart, Armand. 1970. Estructura del poder informativo y dependencia, La dependencia del media de comunicación de masas. *Cuadernos de la Realidad Nacional*. No. 3.

Mattelart, Armand and Schmucler, Hector. 1983. *América Latina en la Encrucijada Telematica*. Buenos Aires: Paidos.

Mattelart, Michele and Piccini, Mabel. 1974. La Televisión y los Sectores Populares. *Comunicación y Cultura*, No. 2, Buenos Aires.

Mattos, Sergio. 1981. *The Development of Communication Policies under the Peruvian Military Government (1968-1980)*. San Antonio: Klingensmith.

Mattos, Sergio. 1982. *Domestic and Foreign Advertising in Television and Mass Media Growth: A Case Study of Brazil*. Ph.D. thesis, University of Texas at Austin.

Mattos, Sergio. 1992. A Profile of Brazilian Television. Paper prepared for the 18th Annual Conference of the International Association for Mass Communication Research, Guaruja, São Paulo, August 16-21.

Mayobre, José Antonio. 1986. *Las Políticas de Televisión en Venezuela*. Lima: IPAL.

Mayobre, José Antonio. 1992. Medios, deterioro social y golpismo. *Chasqui*, No. 42, 24.

McAnany, Emile. 1980. *Communication and Change in the Rural Third World: The Role of Information in Development*. New York: Praeger.

Miceli, Sergio. 1972. *A noite da madrina*. São Paulo: Editora Perspectiva.

Monsivais, Carlos. 1978. Notas sobre la cultural popular en México. *Latin American Perspectives* Vol V, No 1.

Moreira, Sonia Virginia. 1992. Radio, DIP e Estado Novo: a pratica radiofonica no governo Vargas. a paper presented at the XV Congress of INTERCOM, São Paulo, October.

Mowlana, Hamid. 1986. *Global Information and World Communication: New Frontiers in International Relations*. New York: Longman.

Munizaga, Giselle. 1982. Politicas de Comunicación bajo Regimenes Autoritarios: el Caso de Chile. In *Comunicación y Democracia*, pp. 41-68, ed. Elizabeth Fox, Lima: DESCO.

Munizaga, Giselle and de la Maza, Gonzalo. 1979. El Espacio Radial no Oficialista en Chile. Santiago: CENECA.

Muraro, Heriberto. 1988. Dictatorship and Transition to Democracy: Argentina 1973-1986. In *Media and Politics in Latin America*, ed. Elizabeth Fox, London: Sage.

Noguer, Jorge Eduardo. 1985. *Radiodifusion en la Argentina*. Buenos Aires: Editorial Bien Comun.

de Noriega, Luis Antonio and Frances Leach. 1979. *Broadcasting in Mexico*, London: International Institute of Communication.

Neyra, Walter and Razuri, Jaime. 1974. *Situación de los Medios de Comunicación en el Perú despues de 1970*. Lima: Universidad de Lima.

OCI. 1976. *Information para la Libertad*. OCI, Caracas.

Ortega, Carlos y Romero, Carlos. 1976. *Las Políticas de Comunicación en el Perú*. Paris: UNESCO.

Palma, Gabriel. 1978. Dependency: A Formal Theory of Underdevelopment or a Methodology for the Analysis of Concrete Situations of Underdevelopment. *World Development*.

Page, Joseph. 1983. *Peron*. New York: Random House.

Pareja, Reynaldo. 1984. *Historia de la radio en Colombia 1929-1980*. Bogotá: Servicio Colombiano de Comunicacion Social.

Pasquali, Antonio. 1967. *El aparato singular: un diá de television en Caracas*. Caracas: Universidad Central de Venezuela.

Pasquali, Antonio. 1976. *Comunicación y cultura de Masas*. Caracas: Monte Avila.

Pasquali, Antonio. 1977. *Proyecto RATELVE*. Caracas: Ediciones de la Libreria SUMA.

Peirano, Luis, et al. 1978. *Prensa: Apertura y Limites*. Lima: DESCO.

Peirano, Luis and Abelardo Sanchez León. 1984. *Risas y culturas en la televisión peruana*, Lima: DESCO.

Pendajur, Manjunath. 1990. *Canadian Dreams & American Control*. Detroit: Wayne State University Press.

Perez, Carlos Andres. 1976. *Información para la Libertad*. Caracas: OCI.

Pirsein, Robert William. 1979. *The Voice of America: An History of the International Broadcasting Activities of the United States Government 1940-1962*, Dissertations in Broadcasting, New York: Arno Press, 1979. (Ph.D. dissertation, Northwestern University, 1970).

Portales, Diego. 1987. *La dificultad de innovar: un estudio sobre las empresas de television en America Latina*. Santiago: ILET.

Potsche de Carvalho e Silva, Luis Fernando. 1983. Estrategia empresarial e estrutura organizacional nas emissoras de TV brasileiras, 1950/1981. M.A. FGV Escola de Administracao de Empresas, S.P.

Prada, Raúl Rivadeneira. 1986. *La televisión en Bolivia*. La Paz: Editorial Quipus.

Preston, Julia. 1992. Brazil's Power of the Press. *The Washington Post*, 12 December, C1.

Puig, Claudia. 1993. Univision Scraps Three Shows Made in the United States. *Los Angeles Times Washington Edition*, 22 January 22, B9.

Pye, Lucien. 1963. Communication and Political Development, Princeton: Princeton University Press.

Raffo, Daniel. 1992. La Milonga de los medios en el paraíso liberal. Chasqui, No. 42, 65-70.

Rama, German, W. 1985. La Democratie en Uruguay: Un Essai d'Interpretation. *Problemes d'Amerique Latina*, 5-49, No. 78, 4 trimestre, Paris: La Documentation Francaise.

Read, William H. 1976. *American's Mass Media Merchants*, Baltimore, Johns Hopkins University Press.

Reyes Heroles. 1978. Speech, Semana Nacional de Radio y TV, 3 October.

Rocca Torres, Luis. 1975. *El Gobierno Militar y las Comuniaciones en el Perú*. Lima: Ediciones Populares los Andes.

Rowe, William and Vivian Schelling. 1991. *Memory and Modernity: Popular Culture in Latin America*. London: Verso.

Sachs, Ignacy. 1985. Les quatre Dettes du Bresil. *Problemes d'Amerique Latine* 98-114. No. 78. 4 Trimestre.

Santoro, Eduardo. 1975. *La televisión venezolana y la formación de estereotipos en el niño*. Caracas: UCV.

Schiller, Herbert. 1969. *Mass Communications and the American Empire*. Boston: Beacon.

Schiller, Herbert. 1976. *Communication and Cultural Domination*. New York: International Arts and Sciences.

Schiller, Herbert. 1989. *Culture Inc*. New York: Oxford University Press.

Schnitman, Jorge. 1984. *Film Industries in Latin America: Dependency and Development*. Norwood: Ablex.

Schramm, Wilbur. 1964. *Mass Media and National Development*. Stanford: Stanford University Press.

Schramm, Wilbur and Daniel Lerner. eds. 1964. *The Role of Media in Developing Countries*. Stanford: Stanford University Press.

Schwoch, James. 1990. *The American Radio Industry and its Latin American Activities 1890-1939*. Chicago: University of Illinois Press.

Seid, Richard. 1993. Mexico: Much Press, Little Real Freedom. *The Christian Science Monitor*, 8 March, 18.

Skidmore, Thomas E. 1992. *Television, Politics, and the Transition to Democracy in Latin America*. Washington DC: The Wilson Centre and John Hopkins.

da Silva, Carlos Eduardo Lins. 1986. Transnational Communication and Brazilian Culture. In *Communications and Latin American Society: Trends in Critical Research, 1960- 1985*, eds. Rita Atwood and Emile McAnany, 89-111. Madison: University of Wisconsin Press.

Sinclair, John. 1986. Dependent Development and Broadcasting:the Mexican Formula. *Media, Culture and Society*, 8: 81-101.

Siqueira Bolano, Cesar Ricardo. 1986. Mercado Brasileiro de Televisao: Uma Abordagem Dinamica. M.A. Universidade Campinas.

Smythe, Dallas. 1987. Communications: Blindspot in Economics. In *Culture, Communication and Dependency: The Tradition of H. A. Innis*. 111-126, ed. W. Melody, L. Salter, P. Heyer. New Jersey: Ablex.

Sodre, Muniz. 1971. *A comunicacao do grotesco: introducao a cultura de masas brasileira*. Petropolis: Vozes.

Sodre, Muniz. 1981 *O monopolio da fala: funcao e linguagen da televisao no Brasil*. Petropolis: Vozes.

Straubahar, J.D. 1981. *The Transformation of Cultural Dependence: The Decline of American Influence on the Brazilian Television Industry*. Ph.D. thesis, Tufts University.

Tellez, B.H. 1974. *Cincuenta Años de Radiodifusión Colombiana*. Medellin: Bejout.

Tellez, B.H. 1975. *25 Años de Televisión Colombiana*. Bogota: RTI.

Tello Charum, Max. 1986. *Televisión y Radio en el Perú, Politica y Control*. (mimeo).

Tomlinson, John. 1991. *Cultural Imperialism*. Baltimore: The John Hopkins University Press.

Tunstall, Jeremy. 1977. *The Media Are American*. New York: Columbia University Press.

Ulanovsky, Daniel. 1992. La radio como nueva tecnología en las decadas del 20 y del 30. unpublished manuscript.

UNESCO. 1985. *Statistical Yearbook*. Paris: UNESCO.

United States Congress. 1992. House. Subcommittee on Western Hemisphere Affairs. *Update on Recent Developments in Mexico: Hearing before the Subcommittee on Western Hemisphere Affairs on the Committee on Foreign Affairs.House of Representatives. 102 Congress*, October 16,1991. Washington: USG P.O.

Valenzuela, Samuel and Arturo Valenzuela. 1978. Modernisation and Dependency. *Comparative Politics*, 535-557, July.

Vargas, Joaquin. 1971. Interview cited by Fatima Fernandez, *Information y Poder en Mexico*, Thesis, Universidad Iberoamericana.

Variety. 1987. With 21,000 hours a Year, Televisa Exports Soup to Nuts, 25 March, 105.

Variety. 1987. In Brazil Think Novela. 25 March.

Varis, Tapio. 1985. *International Flow of Television Programmes*. Paris: UNESCO.

Waisbord, Silvio R. 1992. Media Changes and Political Communication. Conference of the International Association of Mass Communication Research (IAMCR), Guarujá, Brazil, August.

Wells, Alan. 1972. *Picture-Tube Imperialism? The Impact of US Television on Latin America*. New York: Orbis Books.

Zuleta-Puceiro, Enrique. 1992. The Argentine Case: Television in the 1989 Presidential Campaign. In *Television, Politics, and the Transition to Democracy in Latin America*, ed. Thomas E. Skidmore, Washington, D.C.: Woodrow Wilson.

Index